Dear Blue Peter

MILANO
Scorcio del Duomo al tramonto
Partial view of the Cathedral by sunset
Vue partielle du Dôme au coucher du soleil
Teilansicht des Doms bei Sonnenuntergang

Dear Blue Peter,

Your influence extends as far as Rome. Driving through the city last week, we passed St. Peters. Our 3½ year old son Neil pipes up from the back seat:
"Look, Blue Peter — where the pope lives!"

yours sincerely

Gavin Alexander

1123

F.D.

Fotografia e ediz. riservata GIESSE

RomE 14th March 1982

Dear Blue Peter

Selected and
introduced by
Biddy Baxter

By Lorna and Heather, 1972

First published in 2008 by
Short Books
3A Exmouth House
Pine Street
EC1R 0JH

10 9 8 7 6 5 4 3 2 1

A CIP catalogue record for this book is available from the British Library.

ISBN 978-1-906021-49-8

Printed in Great Britain by Clays

Jacket and layout: Emily Fox
Photographs © BBC

A note on the letters:
All the letters included in this book have been rendered as accurately as possible.
In some cases, they have been slightly cut to fit the available space, but never so as to
change the meaning. The original spellings and punctuation have been kept throughout.

**Royalties from this book will be donated to the John Hosier Music Trust,
supporting impoverished young musicians in the UK and Hong Kong.**

I missed the ingredients! They said get a pen and a piece of paper and off I went. When I got back it was all over. The *Blue Peter* winter bird cake was made and I had no idea what went in it!... Horror!

Well, there were birds out there that needed to be fed. So my mum and I made up our own and I kept a note of what went in ours. The birds in my garden really seemed to like it a lot, so I decided to let Blue Peter know just in case!

"Dear Blue Peter" I started, and set about letting the presenters know what my bird cake was all about. I thought that would be it and went about my life in the snowy wilds of Perthshire, but no, I was wrong.

One morning, there it was on the kitchen table at breakfast. "What's that?" I asked. No one knew.

"It's from London, Ewan," my mum said, "it's got BBC stamped on it."

"What?"

I slowly opened the envelope and there it was. Time stood still if for only a second or two but it definitely stopped. A *Blue Peter* badge attached to a thank you note. I could hardly believe my eyes.

Now the recipe is long forgotten, although I still like to feed the birds. I still have my badge and always will.

I loved reading these letters, sent in to Blue Peter over the last glorious 50 years of her run from children like me.

Well done, Biddy, and thanks for the badge.

Ewan McGregor (June 2008)

Miss Biddy Baxter
BLUE PETER
BBC TV
LONDON W12
8QT

properly
addressed
POSTCODE IT

POST CARD
THE ADDRESS TO BE WRITTEN ON THIS S...

WELLINGBOROUGH
5 30PM
19 MAR
1959
NORTHANTS

Blue Peter

B.B.C   Television Centre

Lond...

LOUGHBOROUGH
4 JLY
1988
LEICS.

Loughborough
Charter
Centenary
1888 · 1988

Blue Peter
BBC TV CENTRE
LONDON

Contents

Introduction

IN A WAY, it all began with a letter. When I was very small, the Jacqueline Wilson of the day was Enid Blyton. This was long before her Noddy years, and when I was five and had graduated from the comic *Chicks Own*, the treat of the week was *Sunny Stories* – a magazine packed with tales of adventure, animals, boarding schools, the circus and Brer Rabbit.

At the beginning of each edition was a letter from Enid Blyton herself, written at her home – Green Hedges in Beaconsfield. It was full of chit-chat and news about her two daughters, Gillian and Imogen, who must have been about my age, and each letter ended with Enid's facsimile signature. I was totally hooked – and such an avid fan it wasn't long before I wrote to Enid telling her about our black cocker spaniel Bess who obligingly let me bandage her paws when I was playing nurse and how I'd tried to brighten up the garden by painting all the cream hollyhocks pink and orange. When Enid replied, it was probably the best moment of my life. She was my friend – so a few days later I wrote again. But imagine the shock when another Enid Blyton letter arrived, word for word identical to her first one! "She doesn't remember me," I sobbed as I ran to my mother.

It was a tough lesson for a six-year-old and one I never forgot. And when Edward Barnes, Rosemary Gill and I were planning the "new" *Blue Peter* in 1962, deciding we'd award badges to children who sent us good ideas for the programme and interesting letters, I knew we must never,

ever fall into the Enid Blyton trap.

This was how the *Blue Peter* Correspondence Unit was born. All viewers who'd won badges were entered into a card – later an electronic – index, against which all incoming, badge-worthy letters were checked. It was time-consuming but infinitely worthwhile. "It was nice to hear from you again..." reply number two would begin. "When you wrote to us last time, your hamster had a bad paw, we do hope it's quite better now..."

The badges were blue, silver and gold. As well as good ideas for the programme and interesting letters, stories, poems, drawings, paintings and models were considered badge-worthy too. To earn a silver badge, viewers were expected to do something different from their first badge-winning attempt. Gold badges were awarded for really outstanding achievements such as saving someone's life or extreme bravery. The winners and runners-up of *Blue Peter* competitions were awarded competition badges and in 1988, green badges could be won by children who were concerned about the environment. In the 1990s it was decided that emails would qualify for a badge if they were read out on the programme or if they contained really good programme ideas. And in 2006 the purple badge was launched via the website for *Blue Peter* Team Players. These are viewers chosen to help the programme by testing new ideas. The great bonus for badge winners is the entitlement to free admission to what are now over 200 places of interest in the UK and abroad.

What began as an act of keeping faith with our viewers (whose parents were paying our salaries via the licence fee) became a rich source of programme material. By the early 1980s, approximately 75 per cent of each programme stemmed from suggestions provided by our audience. It was the most remarkable and rewarding piece of research. The letters – often more than 7,000 per week, including competition entries – came from all corners of the British Isles, and from abroad. They were from every type of home, thoroughly confounding any media studies academics who misguidedly pigeon-holed the programme as "middle class".

It was refreshing for all of us to have this direct finger on the pulse of the children who were watching *Blue Peter* in their millions. The branding, as it would be called nowadays, was a masterstroke and the fact that the badges were not giveaways but had to be won, and that they were attainable by every child, whatever their background or ability, resulted in colossal loyalty to the programme. Audiences peaked at seven or eight million in the winter months, falling to four or five when the clocks went forward and there was more scope for playing out of doors.

It is inconceivable that Independent Television would have agreed to the capital outlay required to set up and maintain the *Blue Peter* Correspondence Unit. The results were long term, not instant. That the BBC was prepared to cover the costs was public service broadcasting at its very best.

John Noakes, Valerie Singleton and Peter Purves with Shep and Jason looking at viewers' suggestions for naming Shep

love letter

Dear Peter
~~thank~~ thank
you for singing
the song I
like as cold as
ice best once
I trided
to ~~~~ write
it in a book
I love you
very much
love Lynne x o

Working in a one-way medium has obvious draw-backs with none of the instant contact children have with their families and friends. It is a great tribute to the presenters that so many viewers have felt that they not only know them but trust them, too. On behalf of our viewers we fought constant battles to get programme material ahead of our rivals and there were plenty of internal battles, too. We wanted the biggest studios, the best filming and editing facilities, and the best camera crews. And once I was reprimanded by a senior admin-istrator at Bush House, the BBC's overseas broadcasting headquarters. Ringing with an urgent programme-related query on a Friday aternoon, I was told by an irate voice: "Don't you realise it is only half an hour be-fore the official end of the working week?"

But when things roughed up, being told we couldn't use studio TC1 at Television Centre (at that time the largest TV studio in Europe) when we'd scooped the first UK appearance of the Chinese acrobats, or we'd had a breakdown in the middle of one of our "live" transmissions and lost a film, it was always heartwarming to look at the latest letters from children who thought of the presenters as their friends and who loved the unpredictabil-ity of the programme. "I like *Blue Peter* because I never know what's going to happen next" was a constant refrain.

There were letters from adults, too, of course. It was a compliment to hear from Edward Sieff, Chairman of Marks & Spencer, after Valerie had told Dorothy Smith's story of the birth of the famous store, vividly illustrated by Bob Broomfield:

Dear Miss Singleton, I have just seen a transcript of your talk on my brother Lord Sieff. It was most kind and sympathetic, and beautifully told. I should like to thank you.

It was through the letters that we began to realise the extraordinary rapport *Blue Peter* was establishing with children. A woman employed as a companion to a seven-year-old girl wrote to say they were regular *Blue Peter* viewers. The child had suffered a traumatic experience when she was three that had resulted in her becoming a voluntary mute – incapable of speech. On a recent programme there had been a film shot at Chessington Zoo that had included a baby seal and we had announced a competition to name it. At the end of the programme, the child turned to the companion and said "Her name is Brenda". These were the first words she had spoken for four years.

There were many other touching letters telling of the pleasure children had gained from watching *Blue Peter* on Mondays and Thursdays; how they'd been stimulated to follow up an item or how thrilled they had been to receive a badge or have had their letter read out on the programme. Sometimes children wrote directly to me. I kept up a long series of letters to an eight-year-old boy suffering from leukaemia. When the boy died, his father wrote: "You may not know it, but your letters meant everything to my son. He looked forward to them right to the end and he was never disappointed. He truly loved the programme and felt part of it. Thank you for bringing some light and joy into his last few months."

Blue Peter is a challenge – children vote with their fingers far more readily than adults. If they're not entertained they switch off or switch over. It has always been geared to the pre-pubescent child and I'm glad to say the BBC has no intention of changing this target audience. The programme is aimed at the twelves and under and that is where it will stay. It's an audience that is lively, enquiring and compassionate, and when the material is well presented, one that is keen for information which it absorbs like blotting paper. It's a compliment to the programme and the presenters that children don't consider presenting *Blue Peter* as work. "Why were your hands shaking?" was the theme of hundreds of letter to Sarah Greene after she joined the programme and attempted her first "make".

There is sometimes a gleam of sympathy. "Were you nervous yesterday?" wrote a nine-year-old after Lesley Judd had made a series of disastrous fluffs. "I know just how you feel. I felt very nervous indeed when I had to read Psalm 23 in Chapel last Sunday." And one gentle rebuke from a ten-year-old that's stuck in my mind over the years was addressed to John Noakes: "Dear John, you are good at climbing and kind to dogs and you help old ladies across the road, but please would you comb your hair."

Of course, there is criticism as well as praise – on the whole more from adults or teenagers than the children for whom the programme is intended. Sometimes deserved and sometimes betraying deep-seated preju -dices, as for example the letters talking of the "myth" of the six million people murdered by the Nazis following Otto Frank's appearance when he brought Anne's diaries to the studio.

Will it ever be possible to carry out such sustained and in-depth research into the impact of a television programme in the future? Probably not. Letters are fast becoming an endangered species. This is particularly true of the last ten years of *Blue Peter,* as communication by email has become the rule rather than the exception. Electronic communication is fast but ephemeral. Hard copies are often not taken and all have to be junked after three months, making life much more difficult for archivists, biographers and historians. There is also something clinical about an email; in many ways, handwriting is a clue to the personality of the writer, especially when the letters are from the very young.

Sadly, this problem was compounded in the 1990s when what can only be described as a BBC paper purge was ordered. A great many files were destroyed indiscriminately and valuable documents like *Blue Peter's* correspondence with Otto Frank were lost for ever, as well as countless letters and emails from children.

Yes, the 50th anniversary of *Blue Peter* is a milestone in BBC history. It's a tribute to the presenters, the technicians, the production teams and the talented editors who followed Edward, Rosemary and me – Lewis Bronze, Oliver MacFarlane, Steve Hocking and Richard Marson – who so cleverly brought the programme bang into the 21st century. But, above all, it is a tribute to the children who wrote in their millions supporting the Appeals and giving us so many of the brilliant ideas that have kept *Blue Peter* afloat for the last five decades.

Here is just a small selection of the letters, and later the emails, that have inspired successive production teams, kept our feet on the ground and *Blue Peter* on the air. A huge thank you to you all!

Biddy Baxter, June 2008

**Lesley Judd with Otto Frank who brought
Anne's Diary to the studio**

The Badge Effect

IT WAS THE introduction of the *Blue Peter* badges in 1963 that started the real avalanche of letters to the programme, resulting in an
average weekly postbag of 7,000 during the 1980s. There was little
motivation for the audience to write during *Blue Peter's* first four years and
very few letters have survived. Those that have show children were keen
to be involved and the age range was significant. The first producer, John
Hunter Blair, had been asked to provide a programme that would bridge
the gap for five, to eight-year-olds who were growing out of *Watch With
Mother* but were too young to appreciate *Studio E* – the regular magazine
programme for the nines to twelves. In the 1950s the idea that a programme could embrace the entire age range from five to twelve years
was considered an impossibility. These early *Blue Peters* were transmitted
weekly and ran for fifteen minutes.

Very sadly, John Hunter Blair became ill with a heart complaint.
He was too unwell to produce the programme regularly during 1961
and died shortly afterwards. By the time I joined *Blue Peter* in 1962, it
had been kept afloat by any members of the Children's Programmes
Department who happened to be free. As I had previously worked as
a producer in BBC Radio before applying for the vacancy, and had
only just finished a brief television training course, it was just as well I
was given a young but far more experienced member of the department

as the programme's director.

Edward Barnes had the perfect background – an actor and broadcaster, he had worked on a variety of prestigious shows, including dramas, ballets and light-entertainment series, and when, in 1963, I was summoned for jury service and the programme lost 50 per cent of its production team, it was Edward who suggested his former assistant floor manager filled the gap. Rosemary Gill was the ideal choice and stayed on after I returned from jury service. It was out of this team, created almost at random, that the "new" *Blue Peter* was born. Together we decided it was essential for the programme to have a symbol; a logo that would not only be seen in the studio each week but would be printed on every sheet of *Blue Peter* writing paper, every envelope and every photo of the presenters. The extended use of the logo would give *Blue Peter* its identity. Above all, the logo would be on the programme's badges. What should it be?

We turned to Tony Hart, a young up-and-coming artist who had appeared in some of the very early *Blue Peters*. He designed a symbol that could not have been more appropriate for *Blue Peter's* nautical overtones – the galleon that was to become the most famous vessel never to sail the high seas. For this he received the standard graphics fee of a few pounds, for which he was immensely grateful. Years later when *Blue Peter* was a household name and Tony was presenting his own programmes, *Take Hart* and *Hartbeat*, we all bemoaned the fact he hadn't been on an artist's equivalent of the composer's performing rights contract. With literally millions of *Blue Peter* galleons bobbing about in homes all over the British Isles and beyond, he would have been the first of the TV millionaires!

There was nothing new about badges for children – they had been around since the turn of the century with a plethora of them as giveaways in the 1920s and 1930s. But what was different about Edward's idea for the *Blue Peter* badges was that they were not giveaways, which would have been largely unappreciated by the recipients. They had to be won, and this was to provide *Blue Peter* with a fountain of material – and result in an estimated three quarters of each programme arising directly or indirectly from viewers' suggestions. The really tricky problem was how to be fair. Although *Blue Peter* was aimed at the five to twelve-year-olds, we knew that children as young as two and a half were avid viewers and there was a strong teenage audience, too. This was resolved by awarding badges for a multiplicity of reasons, not only for good ideas for the programme and interesting letters, but for pictures and drawings, poems, stories and plays, models and recipes. This meant the pre-school child had just as much chance of winning a badge as a thirteen-year-old. It was also the beginning of an understanding of the audience that became unique in the history of broadcasting.

We worked out a system: there was the blue badge for first-timers, with a blue ship on a white background; a silver badge for viewers who came up with a different idea, which had a silver ship on a blue shield; round competition badges with a blue ship and white background, which would be awarded to every single winner and runner-up in all *Blue Peter* competitions; and for quite outstanding achievements such as saving life, extraordinary bravery or representing your country, there was the gold *Blue Peter* badge – a tiny golden galleon in a special presentation case.

The question of how to prevent would-be badge winners from receiving dozens of identical letters soon arose and this is where my Enid Blyton memory saved the day – with the founding of the programme's Correspondence Unit and its record of badge winners. Competition badges were not indexed – we knew that some children would enter over and over again, but as the competitions were different, there would be no possible duplication of the letters sent out with those badges.

Setting up and maintaining this system sparked off the first of many rows we had with the bosses. We couldn't possibly manage with just one production secretary. We needed extra staff and more cash for the badges and *Blue Peter* stationery and this couldn't be clawed back from our budget of £180 for each programme.

There was a frosty meeting with Joanna Spicer, the forbidding Head of BBC Television's Planning Department – the civil servants of the BBC. The planners advised all the programme chiefs and watched the budget like hawks. They allocated all the other resources and studios as well, and their object, quite rightly, was to spend as little as possible for the greatest returns. "It's out of the question," Joanna said to Donald Baverstock, the Assistant Controller of Programmes, and soon to be Chief of BBC1. "If the money can't come out of *Blue Peter's* budget, too bad. It can't possibly be justified in any other way."

"But Joanna," Donald replied, "it's for programme material. If they get the Correspondence Unit and the stationery and the badges, the children will send in their ideas. It's a perfectly legitimate use of funds."

"Well, if you're sure, Donald."

"Of course I'm sure. Biddy's had a marvellous idea. It's just the sort of thing Children's Programmes is lacking – a few guts!"

And that was *Blue Peter's* second debt to Enid Blyton – Donald Baverstock happened to be married to Gillian, Enid's eldest daughter!

At 5.20pm, on June 17th 1963, a Belvedere helicopter of the RAF's 72 Squadron hovered high above the village of Odiham. It was crammed full of balloons, each with a label attached. At the same time, Val was on the roof of Television Centre, struggling with a net packed with hydrogen-filled balloons that threatened to blow away before the countdown. In Belfast, Bristol, Birmingham, Manchester and Glasgow, men were holding down similar vast, undulating nets. All control points were in radio communication with Chris in the *Blue Peter* studio. At twenty minutes past five the word came through: "Release all balloons." And the *Blue Peter* badge was born.

Christopher Trace with Wing Cmdr John Dowling preparing to drop the balloons that launched the *Blue Peter* badge

Ten thousand balloons were released that day and three thousand labels were returned. As luck would have it, June 17th was one of the stormiest days of the year and many of the labels were destroyed by the rain, although two were returned from Germany and one from Denmark. All the people who found a balloon and sent the label to the *Blue Peter* office got one of the first *Blue Peter* badges in return. The reaction was exactly what we'd hoped for and this letter from Stockton-on-Tees is typical of hundreds:

Dear Biddy Baxter,
I am writing to thank you very much for sending me a Blue Peter badge. It has made me very happy.
Love from Simon

Twenty-five years later a *Blue Peter* badge hit the headlines during a fracas involving Liverpool City Council. Frank Ruse, a left-wing Labour councillor, was given a badge when he accompanied the city's Chinese Youth Orchestra which was taking part in the programme. Mr. Ruse was the only councillor to own a *Blue Peter* badge and he wore it to meetings with pride. But a bombshell dropped in the shape of a letter written on headed BBC paper asking for the return of the badge. The letter (which later turned out to be a forgery) said that *Blue Peter* had been approached by Neil Kinnock's office (the then leader of the Labour Party) who were alarmed that the badge had been presented to a councillor with such hard-left views. Mr. Ruse duly returned the badge – only to receive a reply from *Blue Peter* saying that he must have been hoaxed since they had not sent any such letter. Mr. Ruse was furious and instigated a full Labour Party enquiry at local and national level to discover the trickster. He said, "It was a mean, low, despicable trick. My wife opened the letter and was horrified. I was so proud of that badge – it really meant a lot to me."

In 2006 photo ID cards were introduced to end the selling of *Blue Peter* badges online. It was unfair that the free-entry privilege could be bought in this way. So they were suspended briefly until eleven-year-old Helen Jennings wrote suggesting a card – and she also included a prototype design – which won her a silver badge for her good idea!

It's hard to think of an easier way of forming a relationship with viewers than the creation of a simple award, easily won by children of all ages and every kind of ability. Yet nothing totally comparable to the *Blue Peter*

badge had ever been conceived before. It was this joining-in policy that eventually led to *Blue Peter* becoming the most universally loved of all children's programmes, with an audience fanatical in its loyalty and devotion to the presenters, the animals and the whole *Blue Peter* ethos.

Trains – 00 gauge – demonstrated by Christopher Trace on the studio layout, and dolls were recurring themes in the early *Blue Peters*. One enthusiastic viewer sent this suggestion at the beginning of December 1958:

To Mr. Blair

I have just seen the dolls in "Blue Peter". Would you be interested in my Dolls. I have nearly 50 dolls some over a 100 years old. I send you a photo of some of them. Mr. Frank Phillips saw them when he came to Hastings and he liked them. I am 11¼ years old.

Yours faithfully,
Astrid, Hastings

1959
Dear Astrid,
Thank you very much for your letter enclosing a photo-graph of your dolls. They certainly are lovely. It would be nice if we could show some of them on television, but unfortunately we should not be able to show you with them as there is a rule that no girls or boys under the age of twelve years may come into a television studio. I am sorry about this but there is nothing I can do.

However, if someone like your mother were willing to bring the dolls to London one Thursday, we should be very pleased to show them on our programme Blue Peter.

Many thanks for writing, and all good wishes,
Yours sincerely,
John Hunter Blair, producer

John Hunter Blair didn't forget how disappointing it must have been for Astrid not to be allowed to take part in the programme. Ten months later he wrote to her again to check her age.

1959

Dear Mr. Hunter Blair,

Thank you for your letter. It was very kind of you to write to me. Yes I am now 12 years old – I was 12 at the beginning of last September. I would love

to come and look round the Studios. My Christmas Holidays are from the 23rd December to the 13th January. Thank you again for asking me and I look forward to coming very much. I hope you are keeping very well.
Yours sincerely,
Astrid

1959
Dear Astrid,
Thank you for your letter of the 18th November.

What about Friday, January 8th? Of course, you would have to come with your mother as visitors under 15 years of age are not allowed to come alone into the studios. But if you would like to arrive about 2.30 pm that day we will show you what we can.

With all good wishes to your family, dolls and yourself,
Yours sincerely,
John Hunter Blair

Dear Blue peter   1959

                    Thank you very very
much For Sending me a
blue peter Badge and Stickers For
my brother Christopher and my
Sister Jennifer. Christopher is
Five and he is Very pleased.
Jennifer is only 1.year and Five
months so She is a bit too little
For a sticker as She would eat it
I will Save it For her.
Jeffrey Almond (9½)

1968

Dear Miss Singleton,

I am writing to tell you about a boy, Jim Milton, who lives here in Helensburgh. He is a Mongel, aged 20; the younger son of a local electrician.

Jim's great interest in life is the Blue Peter programme and his knowledge of it is astonishing. He possesses all the Blue Peter Annuals. When requested to do so, he has collected stamps, silver paper, etc. He cannot read, and can write only his name, "JIM". As a result he cannot do any competitions although he is under the impression that from time to time his "entries" have been sent to you. His parents encourage him, in order to please him, all pretence.

Jim is never downhearted at not winning a badge or a letter, but lives in hope. So, I asked his mother to allow me to write and tell you about his efforts. If you could send him a letter it would be highly valued.

Jim's other interests include collecting records, of which he has over one hundred. He has also learned to swim – a great achievement for him.

May I take this opportunity to compliment all concerned with the Blue Peter programme. It is an admirable contribution to Television.

Yours faithfully,
Mrs. Gardiner, Helensburgh

1968

Dear Jim,

We have been told how hard you have worked learning to swim. We would all like to congratulate you, and are sending you a Blue Peter badge as a reward for your achievement. We hope that you will enjoy wearing it.

We also thought that you might like to have this photograph of the Blue Peter team which they have signed specially for you. With best wishes from Valerie, John, Peter and all of us on the programme,

Yours sincerely,

Biddy Baxter, Editor

3/11/72

Dear Editor "Blue Peter"
my NANNA made the blanket for
me to Send to you. I belong to a
methodist Church and Cubs, So I do
collect for lots of good Causes;
and always try to help yours, —
but it bothered me to think I got
that badge for making the blanket.
I think its a lovly badge; and I'd
like to wear it with my "guide dog"
badge — but I didn't feel I had
earned it.
          yours truly
            michael.
          (Bonsall)

1972
Dear Michael,
Thank you very much for your letter — it was nice to hear
from you again.

    It was kind of you to write telling us that you hadn't,
in fact, made the blanket you sent. We award our badges
for interesting letters, good ideas for the programme,
paintings, drawings, models and handwork which has been
particularly well made. Because we think you have written
your letter so well, we think you should keep your Blue
Peter badge after all — we hope you will enjoy wearing
it. Please thank your grandmother for all the time and

trouble she took over making the blanket for us — we are most grateful to her.

With best wishes from Valerie, John, Peter, Lesley and all of us on the programme,
Yours sincerely,
Biddy Baxter, Editor

1972

Ladies & Gentlemen,

This is to express my appreciation for your letter to my son David. I consider it most praiseworthy that someone should esteem the letter from a small boy of seven as important enough to receive a personal (not a duplicated) letter with a proper (not a rubber stamp) signature at the end of it in answer.

The BBC and your programme personnel in particular have risen considerably in my estimation.

With all best wishes,

W.J. Carthew

1973

Dear Val, John, Peter and Lesslie,

This may seem very strange but I think I no how to make people or animals alive. Why Im teling you is because I cant get the things I need.

A list of what I need.

1. Diagram of how evreything works [inside youre body]

2. Model of a heart split in half, [both halvs]

3. The sort of sering they yous for cleaning cars.

[T sering must be very very clean]

4. Tools for cutting people open.

5. Tools for stiches.

6. Fiberglass box, 8 foot tall, 3 foot width.

7. Picture of a man showing all the arteries.

Sorry but in number 6 in the list the box needs lid. If you do get them on 1st March I can pay £10, £11, £12, £13 or £14. Send your answer to me,

Love from Anthony, London NW11

sorry the
about
writing **Dear** John, ⊘ Pete and Val

a record → My name is Benjamin Minot. I
⊘ have the most unusual you have ever
herd, and I think I brock a record as-
well.

he, he Here it is! I have brocken 9 parts
of my body. & tells you wh

I brock my pelvis in four places, and nearly
burst my blader. I brock my arm in three
places and my bone came out in my arm
as well. I brock my leg as well. And
to topit off I fracter my other arm arm

It hapened on the **31** of **OTOBER**
and a two to grave stone shaped
skeleton ← like a cross✝ fell on me. If you
are going to have this letter on t.V.
do it before the 18th of may.
Because I am be going
Ben age 10   I come from USA
I like your program

My
adress
22 sheen
gate gr
gradens
London
SW.14
East
Sheen
flat None

All my wishs ~~Be~~

B∞ (signature)

and my
relatoin is
Richard Taylor

P.S. This is **TRUE**

PP.S. A Picture of me is inclosed
and a Picture of nobody.

The record
I think I
brock was
of a get well
soon card I
got alot for
a non-known
person here
it is 42

1973

Dear Valery, John, Peter and Lesley

It has been white in Shetland yes white because only a few days after John went back to London it began to snow and snow and snow and yestarday I had a super time outside with the sledge as there are good hills behind our house. I heard that John had been in Scalloway filming Shetland ponies and I also heard that he was staying at the hotel in Lerwick. We have got June our dog now and a few months ago she got a fishing hook stuck in her nose and on the way to the vet she was car sick. She was much better coming back though.

From Michael, Shetland

Dear John I Enjoyed your omellete very Much. We are Having the SPECIAL Tomerrow Lemon. From Edward Robinson age 5

Thursda October 1974

Dear John,

For five years I have tried to persuade Edward to try an omelette, without success. You managed it in five minutes.

Blue Peter is great.

Mrs. Robinson, Peterborough

"All that day I diddent get a moements peace from my class mates. I thought your Silver Blue Peter Badge so speciall I'm having it framed"

1973

Dear Blue Peter team,

Thank you so very much for sending me my Silver Blue Peter Badge. I was so proud I took it to show my form teatcher. I felt very embaressed when I had to tell the class how I got it, I think its beacouse I'm a bit shy really, I only just managed to splutter it all out. When Mr. Shiply, our Head Master walked past he must have thought we were all mad.

All that day I diddent get a moements peace from my class mates. I thought your Silver Blue Peter Badge so speciall I'm having it framed.

Your Blue Peter speciall Assignements help me a lot in geography and history. Also there interesting factual and exiting, I do hope thair are moar on the way.

PS I think a few of the lads at our school will be sending you sombe ideas for the programme too.

Yours moast sincerely,
William, Blackpool

1974

Dear Editor,

My son William recently received your silver badge. He is writing to thank you. I want to do so too, & in a more general way as well.

We are typical ordinary working class people. Now a 'one parent' family. My husband is dead, my 3 older children are married. William the youngest by 12 years, & now aged 12, is very lonely & has been handicapped he suffered from breathing difficulties, constant absence from school due to broncitious, 3 bouts of pneumonia, & has had to struggle all his school life with something called "dislexia" – putting of letters & words & numbers back to front. We have also lived in six houses, & he has attended 4 schools.

Yet in spite of all this he is now in the top class of a larger modern comprehensive school, a six stream entry. We even have hopes now for "O" levels & further education at technical level.

I & his teachers, have struggled with William every inch of the way but YOU, BLUE PETER have been his INSPIRATION. For 10 years he has watched your programmes, his first words were about you. His motto is "If John can do THAT I'll have a go at... (whatever it is he's having difficulty with)".

He's learnt to see possabilities in every scrape of paper or fairy liquid tube from you. He judges the girls at school by "a bit like Val", "h'mm she'd never be like Val". Peter is the father he never knew, & John his hero.

I've always been so grateful to you. For me, & many hundreds of working class mothers on very low incomes, surrounded by football hooliganism & highrise flat gangs, you are an influence for sanity, self-help & resourceful-ness, you are also a window on "possabilities unlimited". *Thank you all who work on Blue Peter.*

Yours sincerely,
Marion Mitchell, Blackpool

1975

Dear Val, Peter, Leslie and John,
We have a dog named Fluff who plays football and who can header just as well as the dog you had. She is a Welsh sheepdog a bit like Shep but she has grey patches.

Please tell Percy Thrower could he please measure plants and flowers in cms not inches because I'm 11 and I haven't a clue about inches, yards and feet.

Yours sincerely,
Simon, Dyfed

1979

Dear Sirs,
My son Paul, who is 5 years old, asked us to send his entry for the badge competition. I am sorry to say that the entry was not very good and so we decided not to send it.

We have not told him this and as far as he is concerned his entry has come through to you but we would be grateful, in order to keep him interested, if you could send some kind of letter to the effect of having received it and perhaps a Blue Peter badge.

I trust you will go along with us in this matter.

Yours faithfully,
F. Richards, Hereford

1979
Dear Mr. Richards,
 Thank you for your letter of February 17th. I must confess that all of us who work on Blue Peter were extremely sad to learn that you and your wife decided to veto your son's entry for our 'First Day Cover' Competition because you felt it was not very good. We do assure you that we always take the ages of contributors into account and this is why our competitions are judged in the following age groups: the 7's and under; the 8's, 9's and 10's; the 11's and over.

 We are sure that you will understand that we do not feel it ethical to write to Paul saying we have received his entry when it was never sent to us! I am, however, enclosing a photograph which has been especially autographed for him by Lesley, Simon and Christopher.
With best wishes,
Yours sincerely,
Biddy Baxter, Editor

1980
Dear Blue Peter Friends,
Thank you for the lovely letter & photographs and the Blue Peter badge. I was very excited when the postman came with my letter.

My mum will telephone 01 743 8000 to arrange a time for friends and me to come to see the Blue Peter studios.

Lots of love from Roger xxxx

To Lesly - jud, a little
time ago i made the
dolls Lounge But i can
Not play with it
Beacause my
made it into cat has
you can his lounge
enclosed See it on the
took. photos our cat

from amy
and patrick age 6 and
Gordon a ½ years
old.
PS
my brother patrick
helped me make
the lounge he is 9 years old.

20th March, 1974

Dear Amy and Patrick,

Thank you for your letter.

We were interested to know you had made the Doll's Lounge and judging by the photograph it look splendid. It's a shame you cannot play with it because your cat has turned it into <u>his</u> lounge, but perhaps he would not mind if you moved out the furniture and left him with the walls and floor - then you could start again and put the furniture in another lounge - to be kept well out of your cat's way!

Because we thought your letter was so interesting we are sending you both a Blue Peter badge as a reward, and we hope you both enjoy wearing them.

With best wishes from Valerie, John, Peter and Lesley and all of us on the programme,

Yours sincerely,

(Biddy Baxter)
Editor, "Blue Peter"

Encs.

1982

Dear Blue Peter,

Please ask all the children to be very, very careful if on holiday in Cornwall next week and not climb the cliffs or swim in dangerous places or go on floating toys because the helicopters from Culdrose have nearly all gone to the Falkland Islands. (The Seaking Search and Rescue)

Yours Ouin, Woking

Dear Blue peter
When we went
to the theatre
to watch the Ginger
Bread Boy. After it
had finished. I
went in to the ladys
toilets and saw a
Flo. note floating in
the toilet. My Nana
Washed it and dried it
When we got home, after a
family discussion
decided we would
We would give it
to you to help
poor children. pto

Love Tanya and Sonia

-9 FEB 1983

1983

Dear S Kuhan (you didn't tell us your first name!)

Thank you for your letter and many apologies for this rather late reply.

Please thank your father for pointing out our mistake about the Sacred Bow tree. We will make sure we tell viewers it is at Anuradhapura when we transmit our films.

Because we enjoyed reading your letter so much we are sending you a Blue Peter badge which we hope you will like and we are also sending you a photograph of Janet which she has autographed.

Yours sincerely,

Biddy Baxter, Editor

1983

My dear Biddy,

Thank you very much for your letter. I was on holiday with my mum & dad and returned today. I am delighted to get the beautiful photograph of Janet which she had autographed. I love the Blue Peter badge. I will treasure it with my other two badges. I was a runner-up in the Lord Mayor's cake competition. So am proud that I now own three badges.

My first name is Kuhan. My Dad's name is Satkunanayagam. It is long long name. I cant wait to see Blue Peter in Sri Lanka.

Yours sincerely
Kuhan xxxx

35

Henry's Cat with his creator Bob Godfrey and Janet Ellis in the studio

1983
Dear Blue Peter,
After watching tonight's episode, my daughter drew the enclosed picture of Henry's cat – which I thought was very good for a 4 year old!
If you could acknowledge receipt of this picture, it would make her day.
Thank you.
Yours faithfully,
Mrs. Leadbeater,
Kenilworth

Dear Claire,

We were delighted to see your portrait of Henry's Cat and have pinned it on our notice-board for all our visitors to see - we thought it was splendid!

Your picture was such a good one that we are awarding you a Blue Peter badge which we hope you will enjoy wearing! We are also sending you a photograph of Simon, Peter and Janet which they have autographed especially for you - we hope you like it!

With best wishes from all of us on the programme,

Yours sincerely,

(Biddy Baxter)
Editor, Blue Peter

Dear Sir,

My husband is forty years old at the beginning of November this year. I wanted to buy him something rather special, but he allready has most things, apart that is from something he has allways wanted, and tried very hard to get, but with no success. You have guessed, A Blue Peter Badge.

I was wondering if I donated £50.00 to your next appeal if you would send me one. I hope this letter reaches you and if this is agreeable to you I will send a cheque as soon as you let me know your correct address.
Yours faithfully,
Mrs. Pearce, Doncaster

Dear Biddy,

I hope you enjoyed it in Egypt. I did, yes I went to Egypt as well, it was absolutely fantastic. I gave a waitress a BLUE PETER sticker, and he went mad, he showed everybody it, I couldn't understand what he was saying, but I thought he thought it was just a old picture of a fishing ship!!! I took, also, my two BLUE PETER badges. By the way, heres something you'll be pleased to hear about, I was on BBC Radio Carlisle, talking about my collection (BBC collection) and I enclose a tape of it.

PS could you please send me some photos of the BLUE PETER Expedition and a photo of Shep, and of Petra. And about 10 "BLUE PETER" stickers, could you also send me some photos of Valerie Singleton, Joey the BLUE PETER parrot, Christopher Trace, Jason, and the BLUE PETER pony Rags. I enclose 10p for postage.

Yours sincerely,
John, Carlisle
Please hurry in sending. Please give me a ring

1984

Dear Blue Peter,

Whilst collecting letters this week – one very worried mum met me at a letter box in Loughton, Milton Keynes to explain that her handicapped child had just been watching your program and had become quite upset about the news of Janets broken leg; without her mum knowing she had written a letter of "well wishes" and posted it in the box next to her home.

Mum was worried firstly that Joanne hadn't put a stamp on the letter and secondly that because of Joannes handicap the content of her letter would not be understood and asked me to take it out of the box. But after a short chat I agreed to post it on in the hope that you can let her know that Janet did get the letter she wrote. Thank you.

G. Ratnage (Postman), Milton Keynes

1984

Dear Blue Peter,

A couple of weeks ago Calke Abbey was featured on your programme. We have since found out that our great grandma used to work as a Nursery maid at the Abbey over 60 years ago, when she looked after the present owner Mr. H. Harpur-Crewe. Our great grandma is now 78 years old but she can still remember many things about the Abbey including being met at Melbourne Station by a horse-drawn carriage to take her on to the estate.

Our dad has written to Mr. Harpur-Crewe to see if we can take her back to the Abbey for a visit again, and to meet the man she took care of many years ago. If the Abbey had not been shown on your programme we may never have found out this interesting information about our gran.

Yours faithfully,

Melanie Hunt (aged 10) and Alison Hunt (aged 6), Chorley

1985

Dear Blue Peter,

I thought you might be interested in this letter and photo of Petra which my mum received 21 years ago when she was 12 years old. She has treasured it all this time. She was very proud of her Blue Peter badge but some how it has got lost over the years. She still enjoys the programme. Do you think she deserves another badge for keeping these things?

From Emily, aged 10, Isle of Wight

1986

To the Blue Peter Team,

There is a very familiar phrase in your programme "…but if you have a Blue Peter badge and you wear it, you can get in absolutely free!"

What I would like to know is:

(i) How many people have got Blue Peter Badges?

(ii) Apart from competition winners, do any other people receive a Blue Peter Badge?

(iii) As Blue Peter Badge wearers can get into museums etc free of charge, does the BBC have to pay for them? If yes, how much does the BBC have to fork out? If no, why not?

(iv) Can Blue Peter Badge owners from years back wear their badges and get into places free? I'm sorry for pushing all these questions atyou but I am a very INQUISITIVE person!

I hope that you will write back to me, as I can't always catch your programmes! PLEASE REPLY AT YOUR OWN CONVENIENCE!

Man-Hing, aged 14, Colchester, Essex

PS Quite apart from what my name suggests, I am a GIRL!

"I am writing to you to tell you about our villages gala day there is lots of stalls. My dad is usually in the beer tent"

To Blue Peter,
This is a picture of Caron and Evet washing bonnie, and "please" can I have a Blue peter badge I have always wanted one.
Sarah, (age 9), Chalfont St. Giles

Dear Biddy Baxter,
In February 1968 I featured on Blue Peter, with a cardigen made out of Pyrenean Mountain Dog fur. I still have the cardigen and also the lovely memories of that day. Unfortunately I have recently lost my Blue Peter badge and was wondering if I may have a replacement.

I am now married and my husband actually remembers seeing me on Blue Peter back in 1968. He had just come in from school and was waiting for his tea! Little did he know he was watching his future wife!!
Yours sincerely,
Charlotte, Leicestershire
In 1968 I was 10 years old and my name was Charlotte Ball

1987

Dear Blue Peter,
I am writing to you to tell you about our villages gala day there is lots of stalls selling cakes, jewlry, hamburgers and drink. My dad is usually in the beer tent. Please can you come to Kyle to film the fun.
Yours sinserly
Trevor, Kyle of Lochalsh

1987

Dear all at Blue Peter,
My dad has been missing for over 3 years, and nobody has seen him since.

It all started on 27th of March 1984. He went to a warehouse store to buy some things for the St. Helens YMCA and some mothers day presents for my mum. He did not come back home. At 10 minutes past 8 he was registered as a missing person. On 31st March, my dads birthday, the car that he drove to the warehouse was found on the way back to our house.

He had been working at the YMCA in St Helens for just one year, before that he was a minister. The mystery of his disappearance has been in local and national press and we have kept all the paper cutting in a scrap book.
I hope that this letter is intresting and that it earns me a Blue Peter badge.
Yours truly, Gordon, aged 13, Merseyside

Dear Gordon,
Thank you for your letter.
We were all so sorry to hear that your dad has been missing for more than three years and can understand how upsetting this has been for you and your family. Let's hope the newspaper reports will help to find your dad.

As your letter was so well written we're awarding you a Blue Peter badge which we hope you'll like wearing! We're also sending you a specially autographed photograph of the Blue Peter team.

With best wishes from Mark, Caron, Yvette and all of us on the programme.
Yours sincerely,
Biddy Baxter, Editor

1987

Dear Mark, Karen & Yvette,

My son Paul aged 12 was killed last year in a tragic road accident. He loved to watch Blue Peter, and he was very keen on conservation and gardening etc. He had his own small allotment in which he planted and grew things. After he died we had to find homes for 4 oaks and 2 horse chestnut trees he had grown. They are in our garden. It would be lovely if the trees could be planted to replace those lost in the storm damage, and a lasting memory of a precious son. Please could you find a special place for his trees?

Yours sincerely,

Mrs. Collins, Havant

Dear Mark Karen Yvette

We have 6 sapling trees in our garden 4 oak & 2 horse chestnut. My brother Paul who was 12 grew them in his allotment last year. He was killed in a road accident 24 June 1986. It would be nice to know his trees are able to grow somewhere.

From Andrew age 9 and Simon age 5 Collins

1987

Dear Andrew and Simon

Thank you for your letter and your suggestion that the six sapling trees grown by Paul should be given to one of the places suffering from the dreadful gale damage. This was a very kind thought and an extremely good idea. And, as you probably know by now, Lord Stockton would be delighted to accept your oak and horse chestnut saplings. His estate, Birch Grove, was almost completely devastated by the hurricane. I know Lord Stockton has been in touch with your mother and I expect they are making a plan to get the trees to Birch Grove.

We were all so very sad to hear the tragic news about Paul. You must all miss him very much indeed — he sounded a very special brother and son. Your mother told us how much Paul enjoyed Blue Peter and that he was particularly

keen on conservation and gardening. It's very comfort-
ing to think that his memory will be kept alive by his
trees when your grandchildren and great-grandchildren
have grown up! Because your idea was such a good one,
we're awarding you a Blue Peter badge each.

With best wishes from all of us on the programme.

Yours sincerely,

Biddy Baxter, Editor

1987

Dear Mrs. Baxter,

Thank you for your letter. It was a lovely surprise to have a real Blue peter
badge each. Simon and I wore the badges when we went to Lord Stockton's
house on 21st Nov. We had lunch with Lord and Lady Stockton and their
children Daniel Rebbecca & Louisa. We had a good time playing together.
Their have a beautiful house and a dog called Bess. After lunch we planted
Paul's trees and put tree guards on them for protection. We all felt that Paul
would have been so proud. It was a very happy time. We have been invited
back in the Christmas holidays. Thank you very much for finding such a
lovely home for our brothers trees.

Andrew

Mark Curry, Yvette Fielding and Caron Keating in the *Blue Peter* garden with Bonnie, Willow and George the tortoise

1987

The most frightening day of my life.

As I got out of the train I could smell something. I thought it was a firework or had been a firework. After a second a thick black curtain of smoke was coming towards me. My mum thought it was a bomb so she grabbed my hand and I ran with her. The ticket collector ran into the smoke to get people out. He saw the ball of fire and said to everyone "Get on the next train". The next train was a circle line train. My mum wanted to get of at Farrigdon at then get a taxi or walk to the Angel. I told her to go to Moorgate and then change to the northern line there. That was my adventure at Kings Cross station. I wasn't killed but I was lucky

By Jane, London N1

Dear Blue peter team. nIreland I was very happy with the badge I wore It all day. I made an Operations room It was really great. and I enjoyed makeing It. Yours Faithfully Robert

1987

Dear Biddy,

Thank you so much for Edward's badge, which arrived on Christmas Eve and outshone all the Christmas presents considerably!

A friend remarked that the Blue Peter badge is the children's MBE which is about right, I think. We were going to pin your letter to Edward's notice board but it's been read now by so many people that it is suffering from fatigue at the folds and is resting comfortably in a drawer instead.

Yours sincerely,
Mrs. Laverick

Dear Blue Peter,

I am 13 years old, and my name is Nicholas. I just have to watch your programme every week. I mainly watch to see your pet animals, and I love Willow, the cat.

I and my family have 11 pets. We have a cat and two dogs. Our cat is a Blue Burmese, called Simon, our smallest dog is a mongrel, and is called Mutty. Finally, our other dog is a Dalmation, called Kate.

I have drawn a picture of Kate for you.

Yours sincerely,
Nicholas, Epsom

Nicholas Holmes 24/4/88

1988

Dear all at Blue Peter

My name is anthony I have a got the most clevest grandad in the world he has made me a small car which I can ride in, which is a MG when I was 3 he made me a ferrie. I have got to big for my ferrie so he made me a ½ size MG thay run on barteries and james has 3 gears brucks excelarater and light.

Please please please can I come on Blue Peter

Love from anthony, Leicestershire

Dear everyone on blue peter,
I am writing this quick letter to you to tell you that I climbed the great wall of China last September. I climbed right to the top of the great wall. It was very, very long. I climbed the great wall with my daddy and our interpreter, whose name is Miss tien.

The great wall was very steep (but I still ran down and also fell). The great wall lookes like a castle which goes on and on for ever.
From Judith (8 years),
Edinburgh

Dear Biddy
I would like to tell you about
my unusual hobby. I keep a ballon
in the air with my feet wearing
slippers, my record is ten minutes.
As I dont know anyone else with
this hobby. I claim
the world record. yours sincerely,
Toby. James Bennett.

1998

Dear Blue Peter

I would like to say thank you very much. When you said that the Titanic would be on the show I did not think it would be that interesting. You made it so it was easy to understand I felt like I was on the ship as it sank. It was easy to learn and understandable for people my age and younger. I am 10 years old and have started up my own personal project. I have not finished it yet but when I do, do you think I could send it in to let you see? You have got me really inspired. I made my own poem up it goes like this:

> So many screams and cries
> Why did it have to happen?
> All they wanted was a peaceful
> holiday
> Nobody likes getting killed
> So much history
> So much pain
> As the people watch in horror
> Lots of people died

I think it is pretty good but that is just my opinion!

Yours sincerely,
Eleanor, Linlithgow

2000

Dear Blue Peter,

I have just watched todays programme & would like to say how much I enjoyed the show. I was watching when Val, John & Peter put the time capsule in the ground in 1971. My daughter was then 7 yrs & my son 3½ yrs. We have all watched since & now my 4 grandchildren watch & make the things that you do. I hope that I shall still be watching your show when the time capsule you planted today is opened. By my reckoning I shall be 94 yrs. but I shall do my best to be around. Perhaps with Great grandchildren who knows. Keep up the good work. I love you all.

Yours truly,
Mrs. Ingleby, Rugby

Email 2001

Dear Blue Peter,

Do you have any bats in the area? If so it would be a good idea to put up some bat boxes. Have you ever done a show with bats in it? I LOVE BATS, but when I tell people this they just go 'YUCH!!!!!'.

People need to be shown that they don't need to be afraid of bats.

Kirsty Reynolds, age 12

Email 2002

During the article about the new crisp making machine and wonderfull flavours that can be added I noticed that the flavour of peppermint was incorrectly spelt. It was spelt with only one "P". Both myself and my brother Chris aged 11 love the show. Keep up the good work!

Lucy, age 9

Dear Blue Peter

I love your website it is the best site I have ever been on. I am seven years old.

From Sophia

Email 2005

Here is a model dalek that I made with my mum and dad. The base is an old plastic dustbin which became redundant when we got a wheelie bin. My dad sawed off the handles with a hacksaw, the top is a bucket and the lumps and bands are rolled up newspaper and sellotape. The attachments are things we just had lying around, unfortunately no sink plunger but you can use anything really. My mum then sprayed it with aerosol paint which was the most expensive thing but it used less than one tin so we've got some left over.

Tom age 9

2005

Dear Mr. Marson and all at Blue Peter

I am writing to thank you for sending our Thomas a Blue Peter badge. I thought you might like to know how overwhelmingly thrilled he is!

Tom suffers from Asperger's Syndrome and has had a very 'challenging' and often very unhappy time growing up so far. It is a roller coaster existence for him and all members of the family! However, he has recently moved to a special school and has been settled and happy at school for the first time ever. Being 'awarded' a Blue Peter badge has simply been the icing on the cake and we wanted to let you know how happy you have made a small boy. He has worn the badge every day since its arrival with such pride, and it is placed beside him at night. Thank you so much for a fabulous programme and for making children so very happy.

Well done!

The Maltby family, Hants

Dear Blue Peter,

My name is Georgia and I am eight. I have drawn a picture in hope of getting a Blue Peter badge. You see I love Blue Peter and I watch it all the time! I hope that I get one because then my face will match the picture!!!

Love Georgia

This is a picture of what I would look like if I got a Blue Peter Badge.

Matt Baker, Andy Akinwolere and Konnie Huq

The Gold Badge

In total, 502 gold badges have been awarded, mostly to children but also to past presenters and editors, and outstanding personalities. David Beckham and Ewan McGregor, who both won blue badges when they were small, have been been presented with gold badges, as has Her Majesty the Queen – provoking an unexpectedly furious email!

1971
To Blue Peter
Dear Sir or Madam,
I hope you won't mind my writing to you like this, but my grandson David Watson, who is a great admirer of your programme on the BBC1, he a few years ago won one of your badges for a painting. Well I am his grandma and I thought I would like you to know he is now in hospital, for a spinal operation, and has now to be laid on his back till after Christmas in a metal frame to keep him from moving, his mother hopes to have him home in 3 weeks time, but he will still have to be on his back, till march, then have a jacket fixed to him. He has been very brave all through, but a great deal of patience on his part will still be needed, and the time will surely drag. I wondered if it would be possible for you to do some little thing which would I know delight him. I am doing this unknown to David as he is too poorly to think about these things. Thanking you.
Yours faithfully,
Mrs. Partridge, Yorkshire

1971
Dear David,
We have heard how patient and brave you have been during your stay in hospital and all of us here would like to congratulate you. We are sending you our highest award – a gold Blue Peter badge – in recognition of your great personal courage. We were all sorry to learn that you are going to have to stay on your back for a long time.

Perhaps later on you would like to dictate a letter to us — we would like to hear how you are getting on.
With best wishes from Valerie, John, Peter and all of us on the programme
Yours sincerely,
Biddy Baxter, Editor

1971

Dear Val, John and Peter,

I have asked my mother to write to you on my behalf as I can't write myself yet very well. I was so thrilled and honoured to receive the gold Blue Peter badge. I am very proud to wear it. It was indeed a great surprise when I opened the envelope. I am hoping to go home for a few weeks at the weekend. Then I have to return to hospital to have a plaster jacket fitted. However up to now its not too bad. My favourite football team is Leeds United, my grandfather once played for them during the 1930s when he was alive. I hope it shall not be too long before I can sit up a little and write to you myself. Until then my best wishes to you all.
Yours sincerely,
David, De La Pole Hospital

> Dear Blue Peter, 4/10/82.
>
> Why didn't you give Lucy Butler a gold blue peter badge on your programme today?
>
> You always used to give a gold badge to children who had achieved something special. I think having a book published when you are only 12 in special
>
> Yours sincerely
>
> Michelle Gilden
> Age 13.

1987

Dear Blue Peter,

My name is Lucy and I am 16 years old. In September 1980 I received a letter from you, accompanied by a gold Blue Peter badge. I was very surprised when I got it, until I was told that two of my friends wrote to you telling you what had happened to me. On 16th May 1979 I was on holiday with my school and we wandered near a swing bridge on the Grand Union canal. My left foot was crushed in the bridge, and consequently I spent 3 months in Stoke Mandeville Hospital (where I even met Jimmy Saville), followed by many more visits for operations, the longest of which was 14 hours.

Even though the experience was frightening and has left me with some deep scars on my body, it was a great time in my life, because I met so many good friends. In fact I became quite well known in hospital. At first it was thought that my foot wouldn't be able to be saved, but I and the fantastic surgeon proved everyone wrong.

Now nearly 8 years later, I am walking perfectly and am in many of the sports teams at my school, lacrosse, netball, tennis and athletics, and last year I was chosen to represent Hertfordshire in both lacrosse and the high jump. I still watch Blue Peter never having grown out of it. I heard Mark say a few weeks ago that you always wanted to hear of the progress of your gold badge receivers, like me. So thank you very much for the badge, I am very proud of it.

Yours sincerely,
Lucy, Hertfordshire

1991

Dear Blue Peter,

My little granddaughter Hayley has cancer and after months of treatment with dreadful side effects we are told that it has been to no avail and we have little time left to keep our little one with us. She is only 4 years old and has been so very brave all through.

Could she be considered for a bravery award please or could she perhaps be made an honorary member of Blue Peter?

She is such a darling and so bright and intelligent and always so gentle I could write of the joy she brings for ever. At the moment she is very well but we know that this could end at anytime. Her Mummy and Daddy don't know I have written but would be pleased if you could help I'm sure.
Yours sincerely,
Mrs. Brown, St. Albans

1991
Dear Hayley,
We have heard from your nanna about how brave you are. Because of this, we are awarding you our highest award a Gold Blue Peter badge. We hope you enjoy wearing it! We thought you might like this photograph that Yvette, John and Diane have autographed especially for you.
With best wishes from all of us on the programme.
Yours sincerely,
Lewis Bronze, Editor

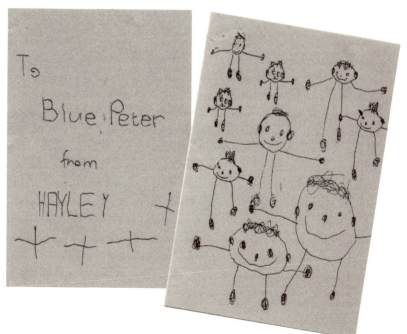

1991

Dear Ms Baxter,

I am writing to you at the suggestion of the Keighley Fire Station Commander to recommend one of my pupils, Amy, for one of your Awards.

Just after 11.00am on 31st December, Amy was in the house and heard the smoke detector. She recognised the sound and alerted the other person who was in the house with her. She saw flames in the kitchen, licking round the doorway to the hall and shut the kitchen door. She ran across the road for help in summoning the Fire Brigade.

Amy is 10 and leaves in the summer to go on to Senior School. She has always been a shy and retiring child, and to act with such conviction and courage is particularly commendable in her case. She is suffering a level of post traumatic stress and is desperately afraid that it will happen again. I am anxious to reinforce the positive aspect of her behaviour and feel that the recognition of a Blue Peter award would be enormously valuable.

Yours sincerely,

Miss Pagnamenta, Principal, Moorfield School

1991

Dear Miss Pagnamenta,

Thank you for your letter which has been passed on to us by Biddy Baxter.

We all agree that Amy deserves a Blue Peter badge for her prompt action in dealing with the fire in her house. We have written to her separately awarding her a Gold Blue Peter badge. Perhaps you could give it to her on our behalf. With renewed thanks for writing and best wishes from all of us on the programme.

Yours sincerely,

Lewis Bronze, Editor

1992

Dear Diane, Anthea & John

I am writing to ask whether you would be able to send my daughter Esther a Blue Peter badge. She will be ten this month. Esther has cerebral palsy and several other problems.

However after watching the skating on Blue Peter she wanted to go ice-skating! She isn't able to walk independently but enjoys trying to roller skate (her dad usually holds her from behind). Luckily we have an ice rink not too far away. The manager and staff were most kind. She absolutely loved it but Les who held her suffered a back ache afterwards! They have told us they will take her again. She wanted to stay skating longer.

As Esther can't usually enter any competitions you have please would you send her a Blue Peter badge for her achievements.
Yours sincerely,
Mrs. Hamill, Kent

1992
Dear Esther,
We have heard from your mother about how after watching our item on ice-skating, you were determined to learn to skate yourself.

All of us at Blue Peter think you are a very brave and courageous young girl and we're awarding you our highest award – a Gold Blue Peter badge.

We hope you enjoy wearing it!

With best wishes from John, Diane, Anthea and all of us on the programme.
Yours sincerely,
Lewis Bronze, Editor

John Leslie

1997

Dear Blue Peter,

My name is Matthew. My mum wrote to you about my stay in hospital. I did not know about this until a member of your Blue Peter team phoned my house to ask what my name was. When I knew I was going to get a letter I was thrilled, but when the envelope arrived and I had a gold Blue Peter badge I couldn't believe it. My legs felt like jelly. When I delved deeper into the envelope I saw aurtergraphs as well which was so exciting.

I am really honoured to have a gold Blue Peter badge and I will wear it everywhere I go with pride. Can you please thank the presenters for the aurtergraphs and the whole team for my gold Blue Peter badge. The hospital told me that the condition I have is extremly rare. I now know that I have something almost as rare, my gold Blue Peter badge.

Thank you very much,
Matthew, aged 13, Cardiff

1999

Dear Matt, Katie, Konnie and Simon,

It was on Tuesday the 5th of December it was a normal day well nearly a normal day and my neighbour was washing up. And I was outside in the garden when... crash I heard a noise. I looked over the fence and through the window & saw my neighbour lieing on the floor I found the door open so I went in and put my ear to her chest and heard her heart so I knew she was alive I put her in the first aid position and went to the phone and rung 999 they asked me which survice I wanted and I answerd ambalance and they came so I had saved her life they gave me a big gold meadal that said "Life Saver" on it.

Love from Helen, Kent

Dear Mr Hocking,

I was deeply upset when I found that Helen had written to you claiming to have helped save a neighbour's life. I know she has a vivid imagination but I thought she realised the difference between telling the truth and lying.

I have talked to her and we agreed that the best thing to do would be to admit she was lying and apologise; she understands now that she does not deserve a gold badge and could not be proud to wear one if she gained it by being dishonest. I have been a Blue Peter viewer for more years than I care to number! I hope you can accept this heartfelt apology.

Yours sincerely,
Mrs Mudd

2000

Dear Blue Peter,

Thank you for your letter but I was not telling the truth. I didn't save my neighbour's life and I am sorry for lying. There wasn't a gold badge in with a letter but if there was I would send it back. I like your show so much and it is sad that Katy is leaving. Sorry again,

Love, from Helen

Email 2001

Blue Peter

I am writing to let you know that I think that awarding the queen the Gold Blue Peter badge completely devalues the idea of the badge. I thought the badge was given to people who have performed extraordinary acts. So I would like to know what extraordinary acts the queen has done. Other than the fact she has had a very privileged life, unlike most of your recipients of your appeals. To hand the badge out in this manor is unfair to your viewers who despite very difficult home circumstances enter your competitions never even get a plastic badge witch was so notably dismissed in this mornings press by Simon Thomas "We could hardly have given her a plastic one" why not give her a plastic one.

Please reply to this E-Mail as I would love to know why she was given special treatment over millions of viewers.

Ian Masters

Dear Ian

Thanks for your e-mail. I'm sorry that you don't approve of our decision to give the Queen a gold Blue Peter badge. We've felt it appropriate in the past to award gold

badges to people who have made a significant contribution to public life and it seemed right, to mark the Queen's Golden Jubilee and her contribution to the lives of generations of children in the UK with our highest award.
With best wishes,
Steve Hocking, Editor

2005
Dear Blue Peter,

Whilst enjoying our family summer holiday in Scarborough this year my eight year old niece, Emily, a Blue Peter badge holder and my four year old nephew, James, were feeding the ducks and geese at Peasholm Park. The adults, myself included, were watching from the benches nearby. James was really enjoying himself, especially when the fish began to rise to the surface to feed. Unfortunately, James' desire to feed one particular fish got the better of him as he slipped and slid feet first into the water, making very little sound. Before any of the adults reached James, Emily had had the presence of mind to grab her brother's hair and managed to drag him out.

Emily's actions helped prevent a potentially serious accident and I feel that she deserves a mention on your programme, as recognition of her quick thinking and concern for her brother's welfare.

Yours sincerely,
Simon Bloodworth, Leicestershire

2005
Dear Emily,
We recently received a lovely letter from your Uncle Simon telling us how you saved your brother by pulling him from the water while on holiday in Scarborough. Both he and the rest of your family are extremely proud. We all thought that this was incredibly brave and deserving of Blue Peter's highest honour — a Gold Blue Peter badge.
Best wishes from all of us on the programme.
Yours sincerely,
Richard Marson, Editor

The Presenters

PRESENTERS CAN MAKE or break any programme and *Blue Peter* has been extremely lucky over the years to have had so many good ones. But, out of the 32 (as of June 2008) during the last 50 years, not a single one has been without his or her critics!

Of course, a change of presenter is always traumatic for children — at least for a while. Not so much for the very youngest: for them it's a case of out of sight out of mind — they tend to empathise more with fur and feather than flesh and blood. The eights, nines and tens take longer to accept a new face and the most conservative of the lot are the teenagers. But it's adults, for whom the programme isn't intended anyway, who seem to hate change most of all.

Part of the problem with teenagers is that they rarely watch regularly. When they do, they want to see the faces they knew and loved when they were little. And no viewers make allowances for a new presenter's nerves. Why should they? Working on a programme like *Blue Peter* is surely one long round of adventure, laughs and excitement! Indeed, if the presenters give the impression their roles are onerous or they don't have total confidence in what they are doing, they are dismal failures. Without exception, viewers believe that any new presenter should kick off with the same standard of excellence as the presenter he or she is replacing. When the departing presenter is of the calibre of Val Singleton,

John Noakes, Sarah Greene, Matt Baker or Gethin Jones, the new boy or girl has a very hard act to follow. Adults can be particularly hurtful, like the viewer who wrote to Valerie Singleton, **"I think without doubt you are the ugliest girl on television – indeed if they put a ring through your stupid nose they could lead you along on a rope, like that stupid cow you are."** Unfortunately, as the writer was too cowardly to identify him or herself, we could not rise to Val's defence. However this request from East Finchley, about Peter Duncan, *was* signed:

> **Biddy Baxter, Blue Peter**
> Please remove the lout who presents your formerly excellent programme.
> **B.S. Robertson**

Elizabeth, a teenager from Sutton Valence, Kent, was far more sympathetic:

> **Dear Biddy Baxter**
> I have watched your programme for almost 12 years now and I have always enjoyed it. It has some very good presenters as well. They're very good at picking up their mistakes as it must be very hard live. It must be hard for everyone involved with the programme.

Very few actors or actresses, let alone non-professionals, could get through nearly half an hour of live TV, coping with animals, nervous contributors, robots, machinery, new inventions and studio spectaculars with casts of hundreds without the odd vocal fluff or aberration. But just try holding a mouse's cranium steady for a close-up, or manipulating double-sided sticky tape and sticky backed plastic without trembling fingers, or cooking and tossing pancakes in five and a half minutes flat. Good presenters make all this look effortless, but it isn't. To add to the tension there's always the need to watch the floor manager, hawk-eyed, for timing signals, check a TV monitor to make sure your close-up shots are clear, and be able to make off-the-cuff remarks in the middle of your instructions and information.

There has never been any clampdown on spontaneity on *Blue Peter*. Some of the best moments have been totally unrehearsed – like the magic moment when Lulu the elephant first wet and then defecated on the studio floor, causing her keeper "Smithy" to fall over when she dragged him off the set. But it is a very narrow tightrope to walk between the snap remark that enhances an item and the crack that interrupts a child's concentration or enjoyment and becomes self-indulgence on the part of the presenter. Worst of all is the in-joke that actually excludes the viewer. Julia of Chessington summed up the tensions in her letter of 1986:

Dear Caron, Mark and Yvette,
I have written a little(ish!) poem which I hope you will read to your valiant editor, Biddy

Disaster for Biddy!
Cameras rolling, ten seconds till we're on,
Oh where, oh where has that silly cat gone?
Caron, come back! Mark, don't fidget!
Yvette sit up straight, you look like a midget!

Five seconds everybody. HELP! Somebody QUICK!
Caron's face is too pale, she looks rather SICK!
Two seconds, don't worry, it'll be alright,
After all, we've rehearsed it all day and all night!

Cue music, smile everyone!
Cue cameras, SMILE!
Cue Caron, no not you Mark
Your bit isn't for a while.

Right next it's the gorilla,
Is his bottle set?
You mean they've just fed him?
I hope he's not full yet.

Ah, isn't he cute!
Uh-oh, here comes trouble
It's Bonnie and her brother
Oh no, the trouble's double!

Who let them loose?
I'll find out later
But for now, am I glad!
It's the end of BLUE PETER!

I hope Biddy and you enjoy this poem, though I hope it's never as bad as I described it!

For the viewers the presenters *are* the programme, and if they don't like them they don't watch the show. Simple as that. Together, the presenters, producers and directors must provide marvellous material to give the presenters the chance to shine. The one thing neither the presenters nor the production team can do is to sink into complacency – the viewers should never, ever be taken for granted. Each programme is a challenge and these letters highlight the pitfalls as well as the rewards!

1963
Dear Chris & Val,
I look at you programme every week because I am most interested in dogs as I have a fox terrier. Acording to my dog book you should not give a dog a rubber bone. It will give them an infection.
Could you please put the matter right.
Love
Marlene, 11, Stratford upon Avon

1967

Dear Val, John & Peter,

On Tuesday we found six salt water shrimps in the River Forth. We're not sure, but we think one of the shrimps has had twins.

From two viewers in Fife

1969

Dear John,

I would like you do a summersault. If not I would like you to show me an alligator I would be very thankful. If you could not do that I would like to see a model aero plane flying very fast.

Yours sincerely,
Logan, Stirlingshire

Dear Peter

I liked when you tried to ride a killer whale. I would like to see you try to skin dive and kill a shark. I have liked everything that Blue Peter has done especially that fort that Val made from lollypop sticks.

Yours faithfully,
Ronald, Falkirk

1970

Dear Miss Singleton,

Last week on Blue Peter our teacher saw you making flowers for Mothers day. We saw it as well and thought it would be a good idea if we all made one for our mummys. It took us all the week to make the flowers because there are 36 of us and we are only 5 and 6 years old. But when we gave them to our mummys for Mothers day our mummys were pleased. We like watching Blue Peter thank you for the good ideas.

Love Infant I,
The Good Shepherd School, Nottingham

Scotland

Dear Val,

The part I like best of your show is when you make dolls clothes. Could you send me a pattern for a teenager doll. The challange I want you to do is to lie on a bed of nails. Please let Danial come on your show again. I watch your show every week.

Yours Sincerly
Johanna
Ferrier

1971

Dear Miss Singleton,

We have all been watching Blue Peter. What a pity you don't do something about your hair. Your face if I might say is far too plain to wear such a style. Can't you do something about it.

Yours faithfully,
Mrs. Townsend, London W14

1972

Dear Mr. Noakes,

The Glenn family, Diane aged 6, Michael aged 9 and Mum and Dad are all "Blue Peter" enthusiasts – tho' Dad doesn't have the chance to see the programme very often! Topicality is one of the points we like eg seeing the Tutankhamun replicas just before the London exhibition opened. However thanks to "Blue Peter" we had the idea of going to Hull, to give them an idea of the colours and size of the exhibits.

Last Saturday off we went by car to the Transport and Archeological Museum and to Wilberforce House which is itself quite interesting and in to see the replicas of Tutankhamun. The children were very silent and obviously impressed, so I tried to explain how sorry I was that we probably would not have the chance to see the "real thing" even tho' we might be in London. To my relief and no doubt to your delight, they couldn't have cared less about the validity of the pieces in front of them – all they said was "Just think Mummy John has touched them"! Alas, poor pharaoh! – John is tops over Tutankhamun!! Thank you for being indirectly the cause of a fine day's outing, long may Blue Peter continue.

Best wishes to Val, Peter and yourself and all the production team.

Yours sincerely,
Jean Glenn (Mum), Sheffield

1972
Dear John Peter and Biddy Baxter,
What's the big idea. Whats matter with Val why was she not on the pro-
gramme on Monday 5th of June and that Leslie was and you never said eny
thing about it. I think I know your little game nothing is the same without
Val there will be nobody to make good things.

Well I no what your going to do your going to get rid of Val arnt you
well if you do you have lost a high grade in children television.
Yours sinserley,
Philip Danielson, Huddersfield
Leslie must not here about the letter

Dear Val John Peter and Leslie
I am sorry about the mean things I said about leslie you see I dident now
that val had gone of on a holiday whiteh the camera team because just after
I had posted that rude letter I rembered that I had not seen the last two
programs and my friends told me. So please forget the letter with the mean
things in I am very sorry for what I said please don't say anything on the
progrmme don't even menthon my name. I am realy one of your great fans.
But I was angry because thort val was going off.
From Philip
I am sher leslie will understand

1972
Dear John Leslie Peter and Valerie
This letter isn't A Militant Protest… because you're all nice and I'm nice and
I love Blue Peter (which is why I'm writing), but why did Blue Peter have
to continue the propagation of the myth that a girl's wedding day is the
happiest day of her life etcetera etcetera (referring to Leslie's bridal gown
bit today)? I know that you are produced and directed by women so I
can't really accuse you of male chauvinism, but isn't it even perhaps sadder
that women themselves continue to propagate the myth when they know
perfectly well – being intelligent and perceptive – that it's a bone-faced lie?

Anyway tomorrow it won't matter, but today I was moved to write this and perhaps Leslie and Val might understand how it is sometimes – I know damn well they must do. I don't often write letters like this – maybe once a year to The Times or some other disinterested party.

My old man sends his love. So do our cats, hamster, fishes &c to you and fellow creatures of Blue Peter. Particularly to Jason: a Pussy Cat to Be Reckoned With no doubt.
Love,
Linda Green, Balham

Peter Purves, Valerie Singleton and John Noakes face a Dalek invasion!

Dear Miss Singleton,

Do please stop doing your hair as if you were a young girl. It is unbecoming, undignified & stupid – it makes you look like one of those cheap flappers.

I often wonder what the Royal Family think about it? Do please look your age when appearing.

Yours hopefully,
HWCC, Sussex

1972

Dear Val, John, Pete and Lesely,

I am wondering how many brothers have been waited on since watching John training to be a Railway Steward. I am one, my sister Angela has waited

Lesley Judd as Prince Charming

on me hand and foot getting my breakfast and tea for me. How long it will last I don't know but it is nice,

Gary, Belvedere, Kent
PS Angela is 8

1973

Dear Sir,

My family and I really enjoy watching Blue Peter, it is excellent. But the last few programmes have led us to criticise John Noakes, what on earth has happened to his appearance? He always looks so unkempt, his hair looks as though he has just arisen from his bed, and his speech is so slurred at times you can not decipher what he is saying, to us he is a pathetic figure, certainly not the quality we would expect from the BBC, one or two of our friends have described him as having had "one over the eight" before he goes on the programme,

but I shouldn't think this so. Please, please tell him to smarten himself up.
Yours faithfully,
Mrs. Duggan, Cheshire

1973
Dear Biddy Baxter,
My two girls aged 9 and 11 years enjoy the Blue Peter series very much, and my wife and I have been impressed with the quality of the programmes which we have seen occasionally. However, in the Roman banquet scene, was Valerie Singleton trying to prove the early origins of Women's Lib, or to illustrate Gibbon's ideas concerning the decline of Rome?
Yours sincerely,
Mr. Search, Manchester

1975
Dear John,
When I heard about your accident on Monday I was rather angry. It always seems that you do the jobs that are dangerous, or exhausting. I would like to see Peter doing some of those jobs instead of you. If I see you doing some dangerous jobs again, I have a good mind to stop watching Blue Peter.
Timothy, Cheshire
PS I am glad to hear you are all right

1975
Dear Timothy,
Thank you for your letter. Please don't worry, I enjoy having a go at dangerous assignments and I can assure you I'm never forced to do anything I don't want to. I do hope you enjoyed seeing the bobsleigh film – I certainly enjoyed making it in spite of the bruises!

  With best wishes from all of us on the programme,
Yours sincerely,
John Noakes

1975

Dear John,

I was more than interested last Thursday when you showed your bruises. I know how sore they are as I am hardly ever free from them as I have haemophilia. I only have to give myself a slight knock to come out in big bruises just like yours. I have been in bed again for 2 weeks as I had an internal haemorrage in my knee. I hope your nasty bruises soon go.

Love from Stuart, Leighton Buzzard

PS I am 11 years old.

Dear Blue Peter,

I thought you might like to know, that when my mother went to buy some citric acid for the fruit ade John made, there wasn't any left. All the mothers had bought some before, but they're getting some more in.

Yours faithfully
Juliet Patterson.

Dear Miss Baxter,

The Blue Peter programme has always been one of which I have fully approved. Our family were ardent viewers and the Blue Peter Annual was a must every year. My husband & I now run a Post Office and sell children's books. This year I am dismayed at the quite unsuitable cover of the book. John Noakes appears to be very scantily clad. Is this sort of picture necessary to attract the young children or is Blue Peter lowering its standards?

Yours sincerely,
Mrs. Penn, Warwick

"John Noakes appears to be very scantilly clad... is Blue Peter lowering its standards?"

1972

Dear Blue Peter,

It would appear that we are to be stuck for good with your new member.

It is so embarrassing for a viewer of any age to watch a young girl badly dressed telling them how clever she is. She never admits a mistake but flounces off, sulks, shrieks with cover up laughter & generally teaches children bad manners, & bad speech. Her sexy clothes one day and rag bag appearance next, with that awful hair, do nothing to endear her to any of us. My son was utterly disgusted with Deadly Dud's (as he calls her) behaviour the day she pounced on the man making glass animals & grabbed for Val's gift. Really. Well what we think does not really count but we've said it.

Yours sincerely,
Mrs. Wheeler, Aldershot

Dear Leslie, Sometime next week if you have nothing to do would you like to come to tea about 4 o'clock or half past. At 47 Woodsford square London W 14 Addison road. And do you think you could bring Jack and Jill but if you can't dont bother. Sighed Heather king.

1978

Dear Leslie,

What a shocking slap-dash demonstration you gave in 'Blue Peter' to-day on how to make Soda Bread!!!

1. You said "4 level teasp Bk Powder" – Your 4 teasps were all slightly heaped.

Use a knife to level any ingredient in any spoon if the word level is used!

2. Fat is cut up with a knife in the flour, partly rubbed in with a knife before using the fingers & so avoid the sticky mess you produced!

3. Why leave all that dough (not paste!) on your fingers? It could easily have been removed with a knife & included in the dough. Use blunt edge of knife!

4. You had no idea of how to knead! The outside edge of the flattened dough is turned into the middle, not just bashing it over & over! The idea is to get a smooth 'loaf' & not one all wrinkled!

5. We saw you put the dough on a baking tray covered with flour! The surplus can burn easily. And we did not hear the temperature or time it takes to cook. Or how to test!

6. Really – !

7. All the same – we really like you & the team & pets!

PS Next time do tie your hair back!

1 2 JUL 1978

dear John Noakes
it is a pity
that you are

leeVing blue
peter because
mummy and
I do not like
changes love
from stephen
Timothy West

1983

Dear Blue Peter,

I have been a fan of your programme for a lot of years now, and as Simon Groom has been my favourite since he started on the show I was over the moon when I heard he was comming to Stowmarket to open a fete.

So I took a day off work and off to Stowmarket I went. I have seen other famous people before and I have been very dissapointed in them as they seem so nice on TV but in person they are very different. But Simon was even more nice in person than I could ever imagined. He must have signed hundreds of autographs that day but he kept on smiling He also had a go on all the side stalls and being as friendly and nice as possible. I would just like to thank Simon, his wife and not forgetting Goldie for making that day a wonderful one for me and lots of other people and one I will remember for the rest of my life.

Yours sincereley,
Gail, Bury St. Edmunds

MRS TINA HEATH,

IT IS TIME YOU WERE OFF TELEVISION, YOU LOOK DISGUISING. HOW CAN YOU BE SO STUPID IN FRONT OF YOUNG CHILDREN.

MRS. TINA HEATH, BBC - BLUE PETER, LONDON.

Tina Heath and Jack

1982

Dear Miss Baxter,

You will no doubt have read the Duty Officers' report relating to my telephone complaint of yesterday afternoon after watching Blue Peter. Simon appears to have a very limited vocabulary and four words are predominant, these are: SUPER, TREMENDOUS, MARVELLOUS & FANTASTIC.

Peter manages to ad-lib reasonably satisfactorily when the need arises, however Simon gets into a total flap, stutters, etc. and altogether makes an absolute hash of the whole matter.

Where have the John Noakes of yesteryear gone, I feel sure that somewhere within the great metropolis or further afield, a presenter of his calibre could be found, thus making the Blue Peter programme a half hour not to be missed by any member of the family.

I would like to advise you that I come from Halifax the home town of John Noakes and feel quite confident that I could take over from where he left off and put Blue Peter back on the top rung of the ladder.

I look forward to hearing from you with your comments in due course.
Yours sincerely,
Mrs. Boocock, London

The team in Spring 1979: Lesley Judd, Christopher Wenner and Simon Groom with Goldie

"Dear Peter, I had to write to you to tell you of the effect you have been having on me lately..."

To peceAr

I hope you are Well From Irimothy Fryer

1982

Dear Peter,

I had to write to you to tell you of the effect you have been having on me lately. Ever since it has been possible to receive BBC1 here I have been rushing home from work every Monday and Thursday to watch you on Blue Peter.

I think what really did it was seeing you in the London Marathon – all that raw strength and courage, plus the fact you have a nice pair of legs! What I am trying to say is why don't you do a 'special assignment' in Noordwijk, I'd be happy to show you the sights, although this may not be suitable viewing for children!

In the meantime, darling Peter, please, please send me an enormous picture of yourself – so I can dream about you every night.

With my love forever,
Janet, Holland

Peter Duncan training for the London Marathon

Dear Sir,

I would like to congratulate Peter Duncan on completing the London Marathon. On being interviewed during the race, he explained how he hit the so-called "wall", and how he collapsed, explaining the reason why Simon was helping him along.

Although, I'm quite sure, he was extremely fatigued since that unfortunate fall, he carried on in that race, gritting his teeth all the way, always smiling.

Well done! Caroline Greenman. (15yrs)

PETER "HITTING THE WALL" AT THE LONDON MAROTHON '82

BY-: Elizabeth Sherwood
Age-: 10

1982

Dear Peter Duncan,

Thank you so very much from each and every one of us in the St. John Ambulance for taking the trouble to say your own personal thanks on Blue Peter today. This to us is our pride and joy and "Thank you" goes such a long way.

Bless you dear,

Mrs. Proctor, 103N Paddington Division St. John Ambulance

1982

Dear Miss Baxter,

Re the recent talk about the Presenters of "Blue Peter". I still think that they are the "scruffiest" people on TV including Steptoe. Surely the people who pay the Licences should have some say in the matter. Even if we lose this argument, thank goodness they will have to grow up sometime & have to dress tidily. (Take an example from John Craven.)

Yours faithfully,

Mr. Lugg, Whaley Bridge

Dear Mr. Lugg,
Thank you for your letter. I'm afraid we'll have to agree
to differ!
Yours sincerely,
Biddy Baxter, Editor

Dear Miss Baxter,

As you say we will agree to differ. I, on my part can switch to ITV whilst you are stuck with this "shower" as Terry Thomas would say.

Sincerely,

Mr. Lugg

Dear Blue Peter Presenters,

Why do you drop your consonants? Is i- a bi- of affectation or wha-?

Yours bi-erly,

David, Blackboys, Sussex

THE ADDRESS TO BE WRITTEN ON THIS SIDE

Bidd Raxter,

Come back, Valerie Singleton & Christopher Trace, all is forgiven. "Blue Peter" used to be a worthwhile programme for children; now it's degenerated into one big jolly party for giggling presenters.

Yours etc.

C. Reynolds

1982

Dear Blue Peter,

As members of the Sarah Green fan club, we would like to suggest some drastic improvements to Sarah's attire, namely that she doesn't wear anything on future programmes. With respect to the 'design Peter's clothes' competition we would like to suggest another competition – 'design Sarah's undergarments.' We are quite sure that, given chance, she would like to reveal all, as she has the most fantastic body we have ever set eyes upon.

Yours faithfully,

S.L. Dowson and M.C. Winrow, Wakefield

1983

Dear Sarah,

On Wednesday 18th April at 12.30 pm I was on a tube train on the Central Line. Suddenly I saw you getting on the train but by the time I decided to say "hello" you had got off! I was very sad not to speak to you, as you were sitting on the next seat. I love Blue Peter and I always watch you.

Love from Louisa, Ware, Herts

PS I am 7 years old, I wish I could help you with the programme every Monday and Thursday.

"Come back Valerie Singleton and Christopher Trace, all is forgiven!"

Dear Sarah,

I am in the Lower Sixth at the Harvey Grammar School, Folkestone. At present we are in the middle of a mock election, in competition with the General Election. In this, any senior member of the school can form a party and run for "PM". I am running for the Sarah Green Party, SGP (originally called the Sexy Sarah Green Party but the sexy had to be dropped due to pressure from the staff). The support I have received has been tremendous and at the latest opinion poll we were 20% ahead of any other party. According to the staff running the whole thing we are heading for a landslide victory on June 9th. Posters from all parties have been made and I have distributed over 100 badges to my prospective voters.

Anyway must go – lots more preparation still to do.

Best wishes,

Pete

Sarah Greene

Dear Sarah,

Me and my daddy think that you are lovely so if you would ever like to come too tea one day. We would like it verry much. Please write a letter back so I now if you are going to come.

from Roger.
x xx

Dear Sarah,

I hope you like the necklace I made at playschool and I also hope it did not get broken in the post, it's for you to wear.

All my love
Timothy, Reading

1983

Dear Sarah,

Will you please answer this question for me? It is, on 21st May, did you go into a greengrocer in Southfield Rd, Chiswick? I saw a lady who looked like you, in the greengrocer's shop carrying some bread. She had something long on her keys and it said on it, SARAH, so I thought it was you.

Yours sincerely,
Sarah

PS Isn't it a nice coincidence that my name is Sarah and so is yours.

Sarah Greene

I thought you looked awful in the way you dressed to meet the Archbishop of Canterbury and to cap it all dangling earrings which should only be worn with evening dress. Your hair always looks a mess and now colouring your nails to show off when you are showing how to make things. You are a smart alec so smarten yourself up, you are in no way attractive.

1983

Dear producer,

Having just watched today's Blue Peter I hasten to write my first ever letter in umpteen years of viewing, to protest about the choice of Janet Ellis as a replacement for Sarah. How could you choose someone so square? I am sure that Janet would be very good for Radio but please not for Television.

That awful 'square' hair style and square frame just don't go with the youthful programme of the last 3 years. And did I see she was wearing a wedding ring? I am sure you can do better than that.

Yours truly,
Mr. Clark, Norwich

1983

Dear Sir or Madam,

With over 3 million people unemployed, was it necessary to give the job on Blue Peter to a married woman with a husband in a good job. Surely there was a young girl starting on a career who could have filled this post.

Yours truly,

J. Humphrees, London

1983

Dear "Blue Peter",

I would like to express to those responsible for the programme, my delight at Simon Groom's coverage of "Sherlock Holmes and his haunts".

I've met otherwise intelligent people who believe that Holmes and Watson were real people, so it was a relief that the programme spiked this myth, albeit in a delightful way, and gave proper credit to their creator. It was a pleasant change too to watch a programme concerning my father which wasn't flawed by inaccuracies. I hope others will appreciate it as much as my husband and I did.

Yours sincerely,

Jean Conan Doyle, New Romney

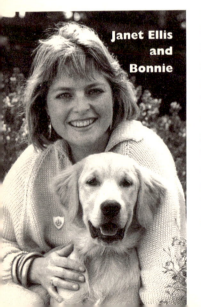

Janet Ellis and Bonnie

1983

Dear Blue Peter,

Rather belatedly may I say how much your "bits" on Mary Seacole and the Ghanaian dancers were appreciated by our family. We are a white British family who have adopted two West Indian children. All of our children watch your programme and its lovely to see more multiracial things creeping in. The way Sarah commented on the dancers hairstyles was sensible and very touching. Please keep it up.

Yours sincerely,

Mrs. Lyn Jamieson, Gateshead

Dear Blue Peter,

I am sorry to say that I don't like your knew TV presenter Janet. I have liked them all since, but Janet takes the biscuit. I don't think she is suited to the programme. You may say that I will like her in time, but I know my tastes and in my bones I feel I won't like her.

Yours sincerely,
Tracey, age 14, Essex

1983

Dear Miss Baxter,

I don't know if you have any say in what is worn in the Blue Peter but my daughters were very surprised to see Janet in something which hardly covered her bottom and I understand she is married and a mother.

Yours truly,
Mrs. Gray, Norfolk

Dear Janet

I hope you are much better. Sorry if this card is a bit late but as we live in Wildenrath, West Germany, the programme gets to us a week later.

Get well soon!
Carol, aged 10

One of thousands of get well cards after Janet's accident while training with the RAF's Flying Falcons. Although she had a hairline fracture of the pelvis, Janet broadcast live from her hospital bed and missed only one programme. She returned – on crutches – the following week. Undeterred, Janet returned to Brize Norton and on October 8th 1986 became the first female civilian in Europe to jump from 20,000 feet. The Falcons wrote saying how proud of Janet they were, ending: "Janet's not just a pretty face – but it's the prettiest face we're ever going to see under a bone dome."

Ten years previously, John Noakes had created another record thanks to the Falcons – a five-mile-high freefall – the longest delayed drop ever made by a civilian.

Janet training with the RAF's Flying Falcons for her record attempt at the longest freefall drop by a female civilian

To Janet
Get well from
soon
Jennifer

1984

Dear Ms Baxter,

Having watched 'Blue Peter' on Monday night and observed Peter's attempt at making pancakes, I would be most grateful if you would in future keep him far away from a cooking stove. His travesty of trying to make pancakes was a disgrace and has set my daughter's cooking back at least six months.

Yours sincerely,

H. Cunningham, Sunderland

1984

Dear Simon Groom,

I wish to invite you to my school's Christmas Production. I am a very good fan of Blue Peter since I was 5. When you write back to me, I will write back to you and tell you how to get to Aylesbury, which is a very nice town.

Yours faithfully,

Carl, Aylesbury

PS You can invite a friend or a relative.

Michael Sundin

1985

Dear Michael,

I think that you might be angry with me for telling you this, so please don't be angry. My family don't like your new hair style. My mummy says that your two front curls are kiss curls. Why oh WHY did you have to have your hair styled differently? I think that your curls before were so much nicer.

Yours sincerely,

Rebecca, age 9, Woodford Green

1986

Dear Biddy Baxter,

Please, after all standards have fallen, do not

stoop any further in employing that EGOTIST Mark Curry. I have watched Blue Peter since my schooldays when Val & Co "starred".

I am not anti-northern being L'pool born & bred, however, myself, family & friends & their fam

ily shall not continue to watch any further if he remains,

Ms Traqire, Liverpool

Dear Blue Petter,

I think that your programe was marvlous with Simon, Petter & Janet. It is such a Shame that Simon has Left. I hate that kNew man who has apeared on T.V. before. He was even making coments about Simon & Goldie. I'me glad that Janet & Peter are still there. MY sister Charlotte Burt has already Recived her badge & her auto grafs, thank-you very much.

Love From.

Miss Alexandra, F. Burt.

Age 9 ¼

1987

Dear Caron,

I don't suppose that Blue Peter gets many fan letters from people who are almost 21 but I just had to write to praise the continued brilliance of the programme. I can remember all the way back to when Lesley Judd joined Blue Peter yet in all that time the quality has remained at a level which makes Blue Peter the best programme on childrens' TV.

As far as my flatmates and I are concerned one of the main reasons for Blue Peter's sustained quality is the presenters which it has had through the years. Although you have only been a presenter for a short time we already think that you deserve to stand with the heroes of our childhood – Lesley, John and Peter. Not only have you done things such as standing under the waterfall that none of us would have done but you have also shown that to be a success you do not need to have a bland accent or wear bland clothes. We think your soft Irish brogue is really sexy and your dress sense demonstrates that modern 'alternative' clothes can still look really stylish. You are an inspiration to us everytime we are accused of wearing strange clothes or are criticised because we have broad accents. Keep up the good work,

Love

Don xxx, Edinburgh

PS Please can I get a signed photo as I think you're the most wonderful thing on TV

23. 10. 86

Dear Duncan

Please please please cut your hair — it looks terrible!

Yours sincerely

The Peters family
(Bramhall
Cheshire)

1987

Dear Biddy Baxter,

Blue Peter was a very good programme until Mark Curry went on, he spoils it & makes it all jokes. For instance on 9th March, Burmese the horse that Queen rode many times was on the programme. Afterwards he said "that made me rather 'HOARSE'". OK there could be a few jokes but not so many as Mark makes. Caron Keating is okay on the programme as she doesn't make feeble jokes as Mark does. Please tell Mark to be sensible if he can. I would rather have Janet Ellis, Peter Duncan & Simon Groom.

Yours sincerely,
Claire, age 9½

Yvette Fielding, Mark Curry and Caron Keating in their tribute to famous big screen legends – Hooray for Hollywood

Dear Blue Peter,

I am writing to give you a tip to raise the number of watchers. Sack Mark Curry and take on the new lass from Ireland. I am 13 yrs old and speak for all of my friends and aquaintences.

From Mel

PS Don't let Peter do recipes

PPS Don't try to dance

PPPS Other than that your programmes quite good.

Dear Blue Peter,

I don't write letters very often but I thought I just had to write to congratulate Mark Curry on his entry to the show. When you announced Mark was going to present Blue Peter and Simon was going I thought Oh, No, not him, he will spoil it all together but I was very surprised with his performance.

Love Nyika, 11, Southampton

30-9-87

Dear Mark Curry,

I have been looking at your programs and I think you are great and brave because some of the things you have to do are quite scary. I've been looking back in the future and since I heard of Blue Peter I have not missed one single Blue Peter program. When I grow up I would like to do what you are because I reckon that is exciting.

Your Sincerely

Diego Cruz

Dear Caron We watch you on Blue Peter,
We Cut out pictures of you in the paper
and We are get a picture of you on are
News Board Pleace send us a photograph
with your signature on it
I am 8 years old, and I an 127 centimes
and my Name is Andrew Orr,
and I like multiply and take away
sums at school and are school is in a
Country.

Andrew   Orr

Dear Madam,

I am writing to give about Miss Karen Keting dresses. I come from Belfast and she is setting a bad standard of our country in England. I am only a cleaner in a school and get a small wage but I can dress well. Karen gets a large wage and I am sorry to say it but dress like a fallen woman. So please get Karen better dressed even if you have to send her to Oxfam.

I remain your faithfully
Ms Ball, Belfast

Dear Producers of "Blue Peter"

Having been retired for eleven years thro ill health, Ive watched certain programmes on TV, but I would never miss "Blue Peter". But since Mark & Yvette joined, Ive laughed so much, they were made for BP. Keep on making me laugh. Yvette's a true double for Su Pollard. Thank you all very much.

Mrs. Tandy, aged 63, Thornton-Cleveleys, Lancs

Dear Biddy,

We must say that we love Yvette as a presenter. She's definitely the best

thing that's happened to Blue Peter since John Noakes.
Luv M. & J. Sibbald, Edinburgh

```
        Dear Biddie,
            I saw your very interesting programme
    on T.V. and I watched it with my grand-
    children.    All three of us would dearly
    love to own a Blue Peter badge but dont
    know how we can earn one.    Would you please
    enlighten us.
            Also, I dont wish to appear a
    miserable old lady, but my darlings and I
    cannot understand the Irish girl on Blue
    Peter and therefore we miss quite a lot
    of dialogue.  Is there any chance of
    replacing her with an English girl who
    speaks the same as we do.   I'm sure you
    could easily fix her up in an Irish
    programme. I certainly would not like to
    do her out of her job.
        We all look forward to hearing from you.
                    Love from
```

Granny Dot. 63½

Russell 8½. Philippa 5.

1987

Dear Sir,

I have just had to turn off your program due to the indecent behaviour of your male presenter. Your morals may be low enough to find nothing wrong with showing naked men on the television but mine are not, and I am trying to bring my two daughters up properly. Please do not try to justify your-selves because you cannot truthfully do so.

Yours offended,

Mr. Millsom, Hants

Dear Yvette,

I hope you do not mind me writing to you but I couldn't help noticing that we have one thing in common, vitiligo. My vitiligo appeared 3 years ago and is getting worse. How long have you had yours and do people nudge each other and stare? I am 13 and quite tall for my age. I go to Barts Hospital once a year but they can't do anything. I belong to the Vitiligo Group – do you? I was wondering if you could please tell viewers about how anyone can get it.

Best wishes,
Jacqueline, St. Albans

It was enormously to Yvette's credit that she said she would like to talk to viewers about the condition she too had suffered from for so long. Vitiligo sufferers have pale blotches on their hands, arms, legs – anywhere on their bodies, caused by lack of pigment in the skin.

Yvette had been teased dreadfully when she was at school and was all for doing anything she could to help fellow sufferers. Together we planned an item involving three of the children who had written similar letters, plus some useful information on the best camouflage make-up available and a general swapping of experiences.

This resulted in a flood of letters not only from children who also had vitiligo but from those who were coping with many other disabilities too.

Dear YVETTE
My name is Elizabeth Glover
And I am 9 years old.
I am writing to tell you that
I know how it feels to have people
Staring at you as I was born
Without a left hand.
It isn't the same as your skin
Disease but I know how it feels to
be stared at.
yours sincerely Elizabeth Glover

Dear Yvette,

I saw you on Blue Peter when you talked to some children about the skin problem you share with them. I am really grateful that you brought to the attention of the public the difficulties people with skin problems are faced with. I myself have chronic eczema. It is an unattractive illness and I still find myself getting upset when people don't want to go near me or hurl hurtful abusive remarks at me and whisper when they see my skin, as if I couldn't hear or don't have feelings. This only happens on bad days now, but when it does happen it makes me feel so angry, that I just wish I could summon up the courage to tell these people (mostly boys might I add) exactly what I think of them. I feel that they are the ones with the illness. I am sure that you have sometimes felt the same.

I think it was extremely brave of you to face the world and tell your viewers about your illness and point out that it is hard for us and ask to give us a chance. Thank you again and I hope you have a long and enjoyable career as a Blue Peter Presenter.

Rachel, aged 14, Pangbourne, Berkshire

Dear Yvett,

I am writing to you after seeing Blue Peter when it showed you with your skin disease. I suffer from asthma and it is miserable. It doesn't mean you can not do any kinds of sport. My most outstanding sport is swimming which is very good for astmatics. Now it seems to me that my astma will never clear up. After seeing the problems of other people I thought I might tell you about mine. I hope you do not mind.

Yours sincerely,
Lizzie, Aylsham, Suffolk

1987

Dear Yvette,

I have suffered from psoriasis since I was born and although it is very common to have it, I was one of the few people to have it on my face as well as arms, legs and body. Especially as a small child at school, I was regularly teased, being called things like 'scabby' and 'fishface'. 'Lizard' is a new one because of shedding skin, and my dad once called it 'fag-ash'. I used to be very upset and loathed going to school.

Now I'm 15 and about to take my mock GCSE's.

As I said I used to get very depressed when I was younger, but now my advice to anyone is just get on with life.

Thanks again and best wishes,
Debbie, Ilfracombe

> Dear Avett   2nd november
>
> After the program today I thought I would ~~wright~~ in to tell you that have Got exma, Some of my friends call me names like "Spotty" man from outer space". Would you please send me a blue peter Badge. because this first time I have found out how to get a badge.
>
> your sincerely
> Peter Abbott

1987

Dear Yvette,

After watching your programme on 2nd November I decided to put pen to paper. You see I get eczema and I got called all kinds of name like Blotchey and scabby. We tried all kinds of ointement which don't do any good. The good thing about it is I cannot do any washing up but my mum put a stop to that by buying me a pair of yes RUBBER GLOVES!!!

Thanks for reading my letter

Yours faithfully,
Sarah, age 12, Swindon

1987

To Evette,

How are you? I hope you are enjoying Blue Peter. I watched your programme the day you told us about the skin cream which one could put on any white skin patches. I didn't quite catch the name of the cream, so please could you send me the name of the cream, the instructions of how to apply it to the skin, and where you could get it from.

Thank you very much.

Yours sincerely,
Deepli, aged 13, Bearsden, Glasgow

1987

Dear Yvette,

I have been meaning to write to you for ages to tell you how nice it is to see a youngster dress nicely, specially on Blue Peter. I have watched Blue Peter since I don't know when. I am now a senior citizen. You & Mark are absolutely delightfull. You remind me of Lesley Judd, John Noakes & Peter. I wonder if it is because you are both Northerners, but believe me I am not by myself, everyone thinks you have done wonderfull on Blue Peter.

Please keep up the good work & I hope you stay for ages on Blue Peter. You know the young children copy you, so you stay as you are.

Wishing you every success & all the best for the future.

Love & kind regards,

Mrs. Roe, Kukinfield, Cheshire

Wishing you a very Happy Christmas and all the best for 1988 also the rest of the team.

John Leslie, Diane-Louise Jordan and Anthea Turner

Email 1998

I occasionally watch your programme with my five year old daughter. Which was how I saw the episode on Rememberance Day recently.

I would like to compliment you on a very well made programme, but there was one item stuck out above all the others.

The young presenter recited The General so beautifully, reducing me to tears. Please pass on my congratulations. My daughter may not have understood the poem but I'm sure it opened the eyes, or is it ears, of many young people to the horrific imagery of the first world war poets.

Again thanks for something simple and brilliant!

Glenn Knight

Email 1999

I would very much like you to pass on my thanks to whoever put together the piece about a gamekeepers work that was shown on Blue Peter a few weeks ago. My two boys were extremely pleased to see it and summoned Mum to watch it with them. Shooting and hunting are very much part of our life and the former provides a vital source of income to the small farm where we live. We are, sadly, all too used to seeing the things we enjoy ridiculed and slated by those who know very little about it and do it because they think it will appeal.

For boys like my sons there is nothing worse than seeing our way of life, work and sports we enjoy mocked and they have even come back from school saying that they have been made to feel like criminals. High quality, informative and balanced features about the countryside, like that shown on Blue Peter, are sadly extremely rare and I sincerely hope that this will be the first of many.

Yours,

T.P. Lewis

Email 2001

Firstly, can I say that Blue Peter has been, and remains an excellent programme. I'm from the Val/John/Peter generation and my children are now avid followers of the programme.

The Queen's decision to visit your programme's studio, as part of her media tour yesterday, was richly deserved. After watching it, my eight year old daughter and I were talking about it. "What would I say to the Queen if I met her?" she asked. I replied "Well, first you'd curtsy".

"No I wouldn't", she retorted, "Konnie and Liz didn't".

What volumes this speaks. A golden opportunity for your presenters to show some grace and poise amid their hectic lifestyle and show some respectful behaviour in the presence of royalty. Instead, we had some half-hearted bowing and a rather feeble joke from Simon.

So often, now and in the past the BP presenters have risen to the occasion. When they don't, it stands out like a sore thumb.

Yours sincerely,
Steve Cunningham

Tim Vincent, Katy Hill, Stuart Miles and Romana D'Annunzio

Email 2000

What a wicked show on Wednesday!! All my friends watched it and agreed it was superb. The reports from San Francisco were so cool, particularly the baseball one as Matt looked devine. He also looked v. yummy at the circus school as well. So thank you all for brightening up my Wednesday evening and my Thursday morning (yes I watch the repeats ass well). Thanx to all at BP keep up the excellent work!

Laura, age 15

2002

Dear Blue Peter,

WOW what a Christmas show! Well done you were all absolutely truly amazing I couldn't believe it! I watched it twice coz it was sooo good. Liz you looked so sassy in the red devil catsuit and in all of the lovely costumes. I also loved your high-pitched squeaky voice. That was so funny I couldn't stop. Connie WOW I never knew you had such a beautiful voice! I couldn't believe it I was soo stuned you were really great. Matt you were so funny being 'big daddy'. Last but certainly not least Simon. Ohhhh WOW! You were really stunning and I was so jelous when you got to kiss/snog Connie!

Lots of love & kisses,

Emma, 15, Irvine, Ayrshire

Email 2003

To Konnie, Simon, Liz and Matt

We loved your christmas at the club blue peter. We think it is better than last years because it has more music and dancing and it's not the usual happy ending for everyone. Our mum recorded the Christmas at the club blue peter and we have watched it so many times the video is nearly worn out! We love the programme it's got so many intresting things. Good luck for the future.

From Abigail (aged 10), Thomas (aged 8) and Andrew (aged 6),
Anglesey, North Wales

PS We hope George enjoys his hibernation

10 January 2003.

Dear Blue Peter,
                I am a 23 year old student and
I still love Blue Peter, so does my mum (but I
wont mention her age!). We were both watching
the Christmas eve special and it had us in tears.
My Grandad fought in the first world war, he
was only 14. He was sent to fight in France
and was one of the soldiers that sang silent night
and played football with the German soldiers.
The way you told the story was wonderful and
exactly the way my Grandad told it to us and
it brought back many great memories.
My Grandad died many years ago, but Im sure
he would have been very proud that the story was
so well told and reached so many people, especially
the younger generation.
                Thank you so much, and I hope you
continue to produce such wonderful shows as this
one.
                Yours Sincerely

                Helen Armstrong and her Mum.

Email 2004

Can you tell me why Konnie is wearing a tee shirt with (I assume) James Dean smoking a cigarette? In today's society when parents like me are trying to set an example, I find it disappointing that this is depicted on your show.

I have been watching the show since as far back as I can remember (I am now 42!) I realise it's maybe an unfortunate oversight, but it's still unsuitable I think.

Thank you for reading this, and thanks for a great show.
Mr. Allan

Email 2004
Dear Douglas,
I can only apologise. Konnie was wearing a cardigan over this T shirt during our dress rehearsal and I did not notice it until too late. I agree it was completely unsuitable and I have spoken to both Konnie and our costume designer to ensure nothing like this happens again.

With best wishes from all of us on the programme,
Richard Marson
Editor, Blue Peter

Email 2004

That's just as I thought, thanks for taking the time to reply, and thanks again for an enjoyable show, it's one of the benefits of working shift work that I can still see it after all these years!!!!
Regards,
Douglas Allan
(an "old" viewer)

Richard Bacon

Matt Baker, Konnie Huq, Zoe Salmon, Liz Barker and Gethin Jones

Email 2004

Dear Blue Peter,

I regularly watch your show with my young daughter Alys and we enjoy it very much.

However, we are most concerned that Liz seems to be spending so much time with cats at the moment, as cats carry germs that can harm unborn babies.

We are worried that this might be dangerous to Liz, and we are worried too that seeing Liz playing with cats might stop others from listening to their doctors.

Yours sincerely
Michael and Alys Bowdery

Email 2004

Dear Michael and Alys

Thanks for getting in touch. Before we made the film with Liz and the rescue cats, we checked with her Doctor that it would OK to do so. As he pointed out, pregnant women need to steer clear of cat faeces but that otherwise, contact is fine. As Liz has two cats of her own as well, we thought it was ok to go ahead. I do hope this puts your fears at rest and that you continue to watch and enjoy the programme.

Richard Marson, Editor

2004

Dear Blue Peter

On your show you were making fairies to put on the top of your Christmas tree. I was very upset to see it was a fairy as it should have been an angel. My dad is a vicar like Simon's, and as he will know the whole point is the ANGEL on the top of the tree, because the angels told the shepherds about the birth of Christ.

Please show this letter to Simon

Yours sincerely,

Elizabeth, age 11, Chelmsford

Dear Biddy,

As a mum of 41 with children who grew up with Blue Peter & who grew up with it herself – please don't change. I heard you talk on Radio 4 and agree wholeheartedly with what you said. Please let young children continue to watch & do makes. The garden is marvellous and pets wonderfull. My boys are 14 & 11 and still enjoy watching. My favourite programme was when Katy Hill spent a week with a family in a tent in Russia – out on the plains – I think. It moved me to tears – I wrote & told her so & she replied! Keep up the good work – don't change for change sake.

Yours sincerely,
Mrs. Fenn

Email 2005
When will Liz be leaving the show, and why does she plan to return several months later, and not concentrate on her baby full-time like Janet Ellis?
Adam Fransella

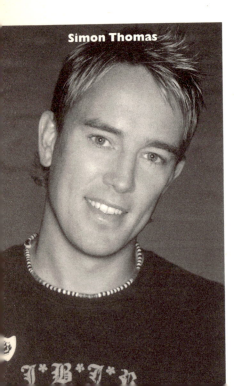
Simon Thomas

2006
Dear Blue Peter editors,

As a 'Blue Peter baby' myself now watching the programme with my 7 year old son, I have to say that I agree entirely with the views expressed by Kate Figes in the Guardian. Zoe's lack of warmth and insincerity is in marked contrast to the other four presenters.

Yours sincerely,
L.J. Eddleston, Beeston

Email 2006
Zoe, Please ignore all that rubbish in the Guardian. You are fantastic and we all love you lots!! Please do not leave BP!!!!
Mike, 53 and Immie, 8

Email 2006

I know that I am 17 but I just wanted to say that Gethin you rock! I watched you run with the commandos over the 30 mile I was egging u on every step. I am part of the army cadet force and I have done a 15 mile walk in 2 days and was shattered so I cant imagine how tired you were. I have the greatest respect for what you did and know that seeing that, has given me the confidence to say 'I can do it', not ' I don't think I can'. Congratulations and thank you.

Hannah Peak

Mahmood Limbada, age 9

Email 2006

Hello BP

Just switched the TV on and caught the last 20 mins of your Wed a-noon show with one of your presenters doing the RM challenge. Absolutely brilliant, totally admired G. Jones' commitment, grit and determination. I served 7 yrs with 3 para regiment 10 years ago now (scary!!) and forgot what was req'd and went thro. He bought a lump even to my throat. But just wondered if could get a copy of the whole prog???

Bloody well done Gethin. He should think of a change of career, it's a good life... lol

Kevin Hill (watching with the kids), Co. Down

Email 2006

Shumae Gethin

We love that there is a Welshy on the show and we love the way you do your challenges. We would like to thank the British broadcasting channel for hiring a good old Welshy so keep up with the good work and hope you achieve a lot more challenges in the future.

Oddiwrth

Cellan and Carwyn Williams

Dear Zoe Liz Konnie Matt and Gethin

I love watching Blue Peter. I watch it nearly all the time. When my mum says it's time to switch the TV off, I say Blue Peter is on and she lets me watch it.

The Blue Peter episode that I enjoyed the most was the one where Zoe was on her life boat saving course because it was really exciting when Zoe went in the boat and it went really fast. I wished that I had gone on the boat with her.

My Mum really likes Konnie because my Mum is also Asian and she thinks that Konnie is a brilliant role model for Asian Girls. My Mum told me that means that Asian girls can go on and have a career and so it's good to have Konnie on TV to show that Asian girls can do it.

By Madeleine West, age 9½, Reading

2006

Dear Liz,

I am sorry to see you go, all the time that I have watched Blue Peter you have been on the show. And now when I turn my TV on at 5pm to watch Blue Peter, I look forward to seeing your face, but then I realise… you have gone!

Thank you for everything Liz, I will miss you! I have loved Blue Peter all the time that you were on the show and now that you are leaving… the show won't be the same. All your jokes and smiles, and all the sad times that you have had, I have gone through with you! So now it is time to say goodbye, it feels like I have lost an old friend that I have known since I was born! Goodbye Liz, I will miss!

Georgina

Email 2008

Andy Akinwolere

Andy since you joined Blue Peter I knew you were a Nigerian, you first cracked me up with your driving test and now I just finished watching the first part of your trip to Nigeria, all I can say is you made me laugh so much!!!

I have much a similar experience to you, as until 2005 I hadn't returned to Nigeria (place of my birth) since I was 4! You cracked me up when you switched from your english voice to your Nigerian one, and then when you showed us your real name on your passport. I was surprised you didn't show your nigerian one!! I can go on and on about how much you made me laugh (especially when you tried to pound yam, haggle in the market and explain the food on the table (odabo!!), but well done for reppin Nigeria and showing the UK how life is there!!

Much love from a fellow Nigerian sister!!
Yvonne

2008
Dear Blue Peter,
I am Grace I am 8 years old. I am writing to tell you that it would be a good idea to have a child presenter because it is a childrens programme. I would like that presenter to be me because I like going on adventures like the ones Andy, Gethin and Zoe go on plus I really like animals.
Yours sincerely,
Grace

To Andy

this is a design I have drawn for Andy.

blue + white stripy t-shirt and shoes.

blue jeans.

from Joseph age 6.

Much-Loved Pets

ON THE LAST *Blue Peter* programme before Christmas 1962, Owen Reed, the Head of Children's Television, appeared on the screen with a large cardboard box covered with Christmas paper and ribbons. He solemnly presented the box to Chris and Val, who cut the ribbon, removed the lid and revealed for the first time a tiny, eight-week-old brown and black mongrel puppy. It was the dog's first and last TV appearance. Two days later she died of distemper.

It was unthinkable to traumatise our very youngest viewers by giving them the sad news. There were just four days for us to find a substitute, so Edward Barnes and I set off in Edward's Mini to trawl London for the dead pup's lookalike. It was freezing cold and snowing. We studied a photograph of the dead puppy as we trudged through the slush but none of the pet shops had any eight-week-old brown and black pups. We drove further and further away from Shepherd's Bush in despair and it wasn't until we reached Lewisham that we struck lucky. In a dingy shop window there was one small brownie-black puppy, shivering in the corner of a pen. It was a little bitch with pricked-up ears and a terrier-shaped muzzle. "Wouldn't you like a nice pedigree puppy?" the pet shop owners asked when we said we'd take her. "This one's really the runt of the litter and it's a right old mixture too – a touch of the Heinz 57, if you ask me."

Lesley Judd and John Noakes with Jack and Jill, Blue Peter's "disappearing cats", Petra and Shep. A viewer suggested the boxes would keep the cats in one place – they were wrong!

The substitute spent her first night as the *Blue Peter* pup in my flat. The carpet was quite a change from the Lewisham straw and, in spite of layers of newspapers, the pup made her mark in every room – especially the bedroom because there was a soppy human being there who made a fuss of her. It was a very long and sleepless night, and the next morning I phoned Edward. "I know exactly how we'll start off – house training!" Not a single viewer spotted the swap.

It was Edward who'd had the idea of enrolling a puppy as a member of the team. The early 1960s saw the birth of high-rise flats and for hundreds of thousands of children all over Britain pets were forbidden. The *Blue Peter* dog would be a substitute pet for them and the lucky children with pups of their own could learn how to look after and train them.

Of course, dogs had appeared on programmes before, but this was the first time a dog had ever taken part in every programme in a long-running series – to be brought up and trained before millions of viewers.

The first thing to do was give the puppy a name and this was left to the viewers. She was given the most popular choice out of the 10,000 votes and Petra, the feminine of Peter, became the first in a much-loved line of pets to be named by children. Right from the start, Petra was to be part of the team. When Chris and Val went out and about with *Blue Peter* film cameras, Petra went along too – whether it was a day by the sea, an archaeological dig, a skiing trip to Scotland or to watch amazed as Chris and Val took off in a hot-air balloon. Like a good family dog, she always seemed to be there.

The training of Petra was very important, if she was going to be a dog for everyone. She had to be a well-trained, well-mannered dog that could be taken everywhere without being a nuisance or an embarrassment. There's no magic formula in producing a well-trained dog – it just takes common sense, hard work and patience.

Children loved Petra. The youngest ones in particular. Mums would write and say: "My three-year-old always watches *Blue Peter* now. She can't understand most of it, but she just adores Petra." In February 1964 we had 10,000 Petra photos printed and said anyone writing in with a stamped, addressed envelope would be sent one. There were over 60,000 requests! The Petra fan club was nationwide.

But she had some enemies too. Many breeders were furious that a mongrel was given so much valuable publicity on TV. The then doyen of dog trainers, Stanley Dangerfield, wrote an enraged letter to *Our Dogs* magazine saying that *Blue Peter* was encouraging "the indiscriminate breeding of cross-breed dogs". Of course, that was far from the truth. The whole point of Petra was to foster care and responsibility. One of the ways we did this was to tell children that, if bitches were kept under surveillance when they were in season, they could be prevented from having puppies. But, if they did want their bitch to mate, it was important to choose a dog with the right characteristics for the puppies they wanted.

Petra

To hammer this home, a line-up of possible mates was brought to the studio, when we decided it was time for Petra to have a litter. It was like a canine "Mr. Universe" parade. As each one was walked before the cameras, Chris and Val would make comments like: "Here's Luke, he's a bit short in the back legs", or "This is Tonto, his tail's a funny shape" or "Bellman looks good and sturdy". Chris pointed out that Petra was inclined to be nervy, so a bold, confident dog would be the most likely to produce a litter of lively puppies. It all worked well, but there were some disapproving letters, nearly all from adults. One mother accused the programme of being "filthy". She said she was so disgusted by this matter-of-fact item on mating, she had sent her fourteen-year-old son out of the room!

1964

Dear Christopher Trace,

I expect you have been inundated with letters with "for and against" mating Petra. I am writing more in sorrow than in anger. The following cutting was published in Our Dogs and I am completely in agreement with the sentiments expressed.

ABSOLUTELY ASTOUNDED

Sir, I have just watched the BBC television programme, "Blue Peter", a children's programme. I was absolutely Astounded to see and hear a Mr. Christopher Trace say that he is going to breed a litter from the weedy cross-bred Alsatian who appears on the programme. A motley collection of dogs were shown for the child viewers to pick one from for a mate for this bitch, whose owners had already stated, is nervous and badly reared! With the newspaper printing articles on the shortcomings of pedigree dogs, surely if the BBC are to campaign for the deliberate breeding of mongrels, at least a strong, healthy bitch of good temperament might be chosen. Mrs. Hill

I hope Petra has not been mated, but I suppose it is too much to hope that there will be a change of heart. Because she is a TV pet there will be a queue for all the little mongrels that will be born. A pity!
Yours sincerely,
Mrs. Robson, East Sussex

The viewers sent in votes to choose Petra's mate and the response was enormous. Armies of people had to be recruited to open the mailbags and sort the votes into piles. On the next programme, the outright winner,

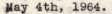

May 4th, 1964.

Dear Sir,

Just having viewed the programme
which is screened for small children
at five ten on Monday afternoons, I
feel I must register my protest at the
contents of the programme in recent
weeks.

It is bad enough to have most of
the time taken up showing an untrained
dog, thereby setting a bad example in
animal care, but surely it is entirely
unnecessary to involve the children in
mating the animal. And I could hardly
believe my ears when the programme
began this afternoon and the question
of whether the animal was having puppies
or not was discussed.

I am all in favour of children
knowing the facts of life, both human
and animal, but there is a time and
place for everything and I feel it is
no part of the B.B.C.'s job to bring
it into such prominence. The childrens
programmes should be purely for
entertainment, there are adequate
facilities in the Schools Broadcasts
for any educating which it is felt to
be needed.

I hope that mine is not the only
voice to be raised in protest and hope
that in future the programme will revert
to being what it purports to be - a
magazine programme for the younger
viewer, not a thinly disguised nature
lesson.

Yours faithfully,

Beryl Smith

Bellman the Beagle, was declared. He and Petra were duly mated and everyone sat back to await the results. Eventually the vet did some tests and gave us the dismal result – "I'm afraid there's nothing doing," he said. "I can't believe it," said Val, "not after all those votes and everything." "Well," said the vet, "all I can tell you is that the bitch is not in whelp and what's more, I doubt she ever will be."

1964

Dear Sir,

As a grandmother I am writing to you to say I think you should be a little more discreet about the vet feeling Petra's stomach for puppies. It was only a short time ago you asked children to pick a husband for her and as it is a childs programme they ask some funny questions.

Yours Truly,

Mrs. Brock, Bristol

Of course, we had to break the bad news and it was only after we'd given up all hope of Petra ever producing puppies that the unexpected happened – and all quite by chance. A friend of our dog adviser owned a four-year-old Shetland sheepdog, Moss. Physically and temperamentally, Moss and Petra made a good match, and Thursday September 9th 1965 became one of *Blue Peter's* most important anniversaries, when Petra gave birth to eight puppies at half past three in the afternoon. There were seven dogs and one bitch and all eight were healthy. Within days we filmed them – to the delight of the viewers – apart from one furious parent who wrote to the Director-General complaining that Petra had been seen suckling her pups, which she described as "an obscenity".

The puppies made a huge impact on the press. Reporters rang the office constantly and all the national newspapers demanded photographs. Twelve days later, when the puppies came to the studio, Petra had her first-ever press call and the next day there was a double-page spread in the *Daily Express,* large photographs in the *Daily Mirror* and the *London Evening*

Petra's puppies make their first appearance on the programme together with their father, Moss

News and in provincial papers all over the UK. But this was nothing compared with the reaction from *Blue Peter* viewers. Once again, letters and cards arrived by the sackful. The puppies were just as popular as Petra and there were hundreds of requests by every post: "Please, please can I have one of Petra's puppies?", "We have a big garden and I'd love to give one of the puppies a home", and "My mum says it's quite alright if I have a puppy, so I'll come on Friday and choose one"!

In the end we decided to give all but one of the pups to people or places where they would lead useful, working lives. Candy, Peter and Kim went to children's homes; Prince, the smallest, to an old people's home. Rex and Bruce went to farms to become sheep and cattle dogs. Rover, the

"Dear Petra, I would like you to come to my party if it is possible..."

largest, became a regimental mascot, and we decided to keep Patch as a *Blue Peter* dog.

Petra's fame and popularity grew and grew. Fifteen years later, when she died, she received press, radio and TV coverage like no other dog before or since. We had been able to make her illness and her death a very real lesson in life for the many children who might sooner or later be facing the same situation with their own pets. As well as her rheumatic back legs and failing sight, Petra had also been diagnosed as diabetic. We had made no secret of this and the news seemed to give children who also suffered from diabetes a great deal of encouragement. This letter from a ten-year-old boy was typical of the many we received:

> **Dear Blue Peter,**
> I have just found out that Petra has diabetes. I found out I had it two weeks ago and I had to go into hospital. I have one jab of insulin in the morning. Could you please tell me does Petra have a jab, take pills or is she just on a special diet?

In May 1977, this invitation from Redcar arrived:

> **Dear Petra,**
> My name is Nicholas Wighton and I am six years old. I only heard the other day that you are diabetic. I am diabetic as well as you and on May 29th my mummy is having a Jubilee party just for diabetic children so that we don't feel left out of the celebrations. I would like you to come to my party if it is possible. My mummy will give you your injection.
> **Lots of love, Nicholas**

We accepted Nicholas's kind invitation and the party marking the Queen's Silver Jubilee was a huge success. The local paper, the *Evening Gazette,* was there to take photographs, the local council chipped in with Jubilee flags and kindly shopkeepers sent free milk and diabetic foods.

For Nicholas and his friends it was the party of a lifetime. For the programme it was a poignant reminder that, old and ill as she was, Petra still had a very special place in the hearts of even the youngest viewer. But we knew it was becoming increasingly unfair to subject her to the upheaval of studio appearances. We wanted to break the news gently so we threw out a hint on the programme before we announced her retirement. The presenters asked viewers to watch on June 30th as there would be some important news about Petra. But this backfired, and by the following post we had some agonised appeals.

To all at Blue Peter
PLEASE, PLEASE DO NOT HAVE PETRA PUT TO SLEEP because she is old, because we love her. You are going to tell us something horrible on Thursday, we know you are. PLEASE, PLEASE DO NOT TAKE HER LOVELY LIFE, WE LOVE HER.

This letter convinced us that to avoid millions more children being deeply upset, we would have to word Petra's retirement announcement very, very carefully. Judging by the next load of Petra post, we got it right. Viewers wrote to say they accepted that retirement was the best move, like five-year-old Julie:

Dear Blue Peter,
I am very sad for Petra not to be going on television. I hope she likes it at the farm
Love from Julie xxx

We were surprised and touched by the number of teenagers who wrote, like this sixteen-year-old boy from Nottingham:

Dear all,
I must write to express my sorrow over Petra's retirement although I agree,

after reading the paper and seeing the programme, it is only fair and fitting that such a fine old lady should retire to the quiet during her later years of life. The length of time she has lived only underlines how well she has been looked after. I salute a grand old lady.

PS I left work at 4.30 pm instead of 5pm to see the programme on June 30th.

There were letters from pensioners, shiftworkers, au pair girls and the children who first saw Petra on *Blue Peter* when they were little, some of whom were now watching with children of their own.

Dear Lesley, Pete and John,

I would just like to say how sorry I am that Petra is going to be retired.

I am 21 and was one of those five-year-olds that you mentioned, when Petra first joined Blue Peter. Please keep us up to date on how Petra gets on as she is very special to me; tears came to my eyes when Pete announced on TV that she was going.

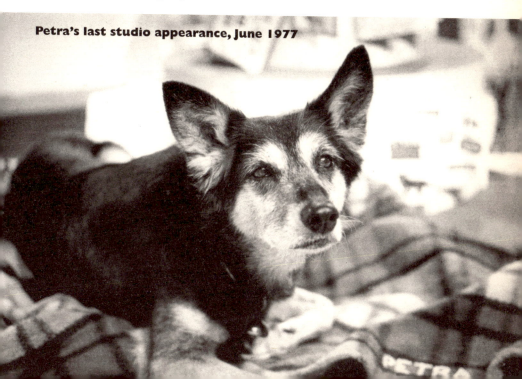

Petra's last studio appearance, June 1977

We had every intention of keeping viewers in touch with Petra. During the summer break she was filmed in the garden where the other *Blue Peter* animals were staying with Edith Menezes, a great friend of the programme and a world-famous cat breeder and international judge. Little did we know then that it would be the last of Petra's 1,122 *Blue Peter* appearances. When the programme returned after the break, we said how weak Petra had become, so frail she couldn't even move to urinate. We asked Edith to take her to the vet to be put to sleep quickly and painlessly. Petra ended her life peacefully, aged fourteen years, ten months and twenty days.

That morning the BBC Press Office put out a release, and within an hour, news of Petra's death had been announced on all the radio news bulletins. Even the Radio 1 rock shows had carried the newsflash. For the rest of the day there was chaos in the *Blue Peter* office with every single one of the twenty-odd telephone extensions ringing at once. The calls came from every corner of the country, from newspaper reporters, magazines, local broadcasting stations, from children and from adults.

Even though we knew Petra was popular, we were quite unprepared for the flood of feeling and interest and for the sympathy and thoughtfulness expressed by callers. We manned the office throughout the lunch hour, thanked all those who rang up, sent off dozens of photographs to the clamouring newspaper picture editors and rewrote the script for Thursday's programme.

It was touching to hear weatherman Michael Fish pay tribute to Petra and John Craven make appreciative comments on *Newsround*. Petra was mentioned on the early evening television news too. Just before that, we had had an animal taxidermist on the line, hoping he could send a refrigerated van for Petra's body so that it could be stuffed and put on public display! Five proprietors of pet cemeteries offered free plots for Petra's grave. But we had promised Edith long ago that when Petra died she could be buried in her garden.

By Thursday's programme, Petra was news in every single national paper and in every provincial paper too. We were immensely grateful for all the press and TV coverage because we wanted to do all we could to soften the blow of giving the news of Petra's death on *Blue Peter* itself.

Afterwards, the presenters said they had never been so nervous. "It was knowing I mustn't make a mistake that terrified me," said Peter Purves. "I was literally shaking all through the programme."

Within a week, we had received 40,000 requests for Petra's photograph and they were still coming in two months later. About half the letters asked if it would be possible to have a statue erected in Petra's honour, and the artist William Timyn, who years earlier had made a small sculpture of Petra, suggested that he might sculpt a new and much larger bronze to be put up outside Television Centre for everyone to see. For some years now it has had pride of place in the Blue Peter garden.

The sculptor William Timyn with his Petra sketches for his commemorative bronze bust

Petra had undoubtedly made history in a way we never dreamed would be possible. She was loved not only by us, but by millions of others. In terms of the sheer pleasure she gave to children and adults in a turbulent and often frightening world, she truly was a dog for everyone.

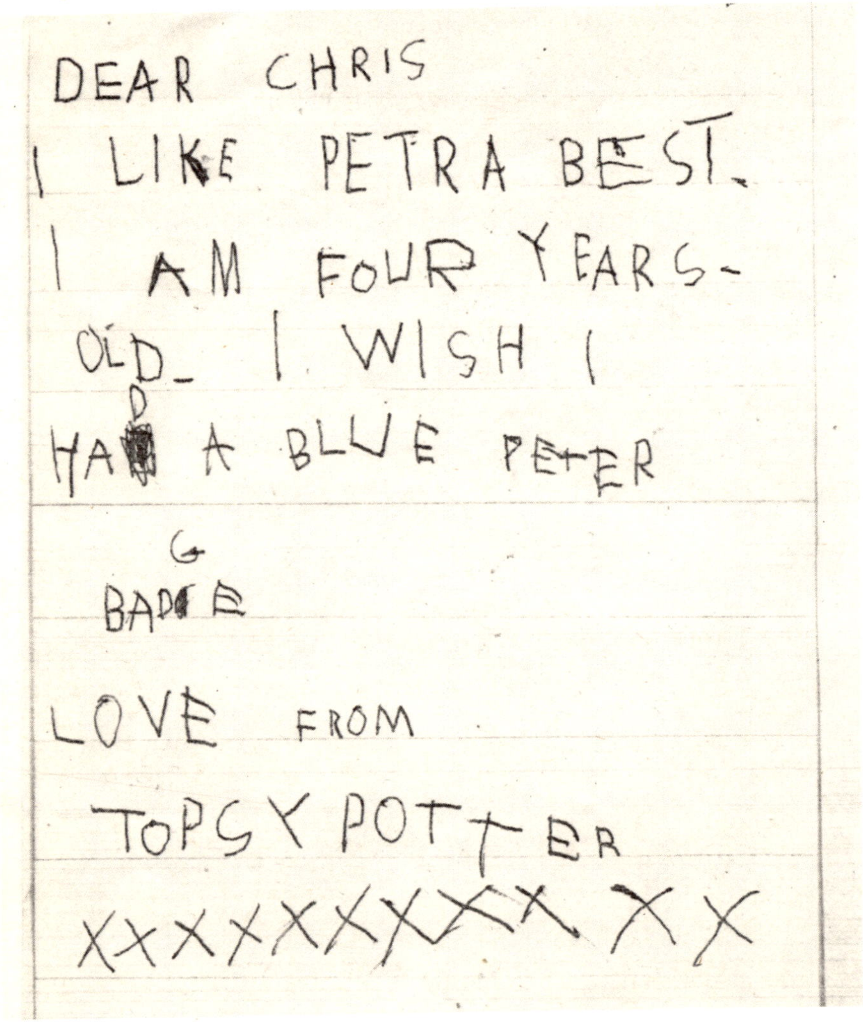

DEAR CHRIS
I LIKE PETRA BEST.
I AM FOUR YEARS-
OLD. I WISH I
HAD A BLUE PETER

BADGE

LOVE FROM

TOPSY POTTER
XXXXXXXX XX

1977

Dear Blue Peter,

When my mum, three brothers and I saw your programme today we thought you should have a statue of PETRA, not just her head but the whole of her lying down on a slab so that you will remember more what she looks like.

Yours truly,

Rebecca, Northumberland

Fred the tortoise joined the programme in October 1963. An "A" was added to his name a few years later when zoologist George Cansdale confirmed what a sharp-eyed viewer suspected – that he was a she.

Our first cat, Jason, was the result of a letter a year later from twelve-year-old Bridget who wrote saying, "Now you've got a dog on the programme wouldn't you like a cat as well? Our Seal Point Siamese has just had kittens and we'd like you to have one." Jason made his first visit to the studio when he was three weeks old, together with his mother's brother and sister. He joined the team permanently when he had had his vaccinations and, like Petra, his name was chosen by *Blue Peter* viewers. We showed his upbringing and his training, and gradually he and Petra established an uneasy truce.

There was a sweet pussy called Jason,
Whose bed was a washing-up basin.
And he said 'It's a fine
Little place to recline,
And to spend the rest of my days in.
Fiona Roberts

Age 12½

Val with Jason

Jason was exceptionally well behaved in the studio. Indeed, he sat so still on his cushion that one old lady wrote: "It is quite obvious you're giving your cat aspirin tablets. This is a very cruel thing to do." The thought had never crossed our minds, but the viewer remained unconvinced.

There have been 24 pets since Petra made her first appearance. Some of their deaths, like Petra's, happened naturally; others were from unexpected illnesses or accidents. Our only real failures were the parrots. Joey, a blue-fronted Brazilian, chosen and named as a result of a competition in the second *Blue Peter* book, caught an infection and died in 1968. But we had even worse luck with Barney, who succeeded him and who died of a rare lung disease.

Petra's puppy Patch, who made a great double act with John Noakes, died of the very rare disease, E. coli septicaemia, when he was only five years old. But his successor, Shep, the Border collie, lived to be sixteen. Shep was a tremendous character and had star billing with John in the series *Go With Noakes*, often called *Go With Shep*. It was a great honour when The Barron Knights, a comedy rock group, wrote a song called "Get Down Shep", which was a rollicking John and Shep send-up.

Ever since Petra, pets have been a popular and very important ingredient of the programme. The full cast list is at the back of this book. Here is some of the fan mail – and some criticism too!

Patch

1971

Dear John Noakes

Simon saw Patch's photograph in the paper this morning and was very upset when we told him the sad news – as indeed we all were. He said that he wanted to write to you, so he told me what he wanted to say and I wrote it out for him to copy. The words and the writing are his own, and this is the first letter he was ever written — he was four years old last month. I should like to take this opportunity of expressing my gratitude to the whole Blue Peter programme team for the sustained interest and pleasure provided by your programme; Simon and I enjoy it immensely and his baby brother Benjamin is being brought up on twice-weekly doses of "Blue Peter". Simon's appreciation of nature has been greatly enhanced by your features on animals, and his social conscience sharpened by the "Blue Peter" appeals — the family was recently stripped of all unwanted forks and spoons!

Patch, with his lively, mischievous personality, will be sadly missed by us all, and we offer our sincere sympathy at his untimely death.

With best wishes,
Mrs. Michaelis, Woking

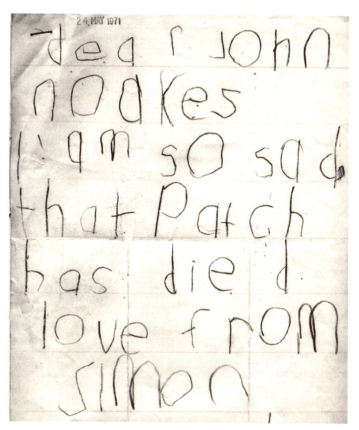

1971

Dear John, Val and Peter,

I have been in Zambia just a fortnight and I was very upset to read in the Daily Telegraph that Patch, John Noakes dog has died.

We were very devoted viewers of Blue Peter when we were in England. We are here for two years and we miss you.

I think all your programmes are very interesting. I like the programmes when Val makes things. I wish that the programme could be transmitted out here.

Yours faithfully,
Denise Turrell

1978

Dear Simon, Lesley and John

Do you remember me. I wrote that letter about Jason the cat when he died and you sent me a photo of him. Well I have kept it from 1976. I hope you are well down in London I am saying down in London because I have moved up North now and I am a weekly border at Heathfield School.

Lots of love from
Charlotte, Bradford

xxxxxxxxxxxxxxxx

PS I hope Jack and Jill are well

1980

Dear Blue Peter,

Please could you find a mate for Goldie so she can have pups like you did with Petra?

If you gave a list of the dogs and showed them on the programme us viewers could vote for the one we want. Personally I like a Border Collie best.

Yours hopefully,
Anna, Buckingham

Viewers sent Jason hundreds of cards for his tenth birthday

1982

Dear Blue Peter,

My name is Andrew I attend an adult training centre for the mentally handi-capped. I am 24 years old. I have watched your programme for many years and have always enjoyed it.

I would love to see a flashback of Goldies puppies again. I loved your programme with the Austin 7. My uncle has one also and he has promised me a ride in it soon.

Best wishes,
Andrew, Bristol

**Goldie and her second litter.
All eight pups became guide
dogs – Prince, the puppy walked
by Peter Duncan, is yawning!**

Jack and Jill were the two silver-spotted tabby kittens that took over from Jason in 1976. They soon became known as the disappearing cats!

1983

The Editor, Radio Times
Dear Sir,

There is much to admire in Blue Peter but yesterday it reached the depths of inanity with the preposterous celebration of the birthday of two cats whose appearances have never been more than minimal and whose indifference to the proceedings are monumental. Might I suggest that to assuage the disgust of many cat lovers these two ill-tempered moggies are put to a better (and distant) use? A roving holiday in the Falkland Islands would, I think, provide them with a setting far more suitable to their truculent qualities.

And, incidentally, I am surprised that viewers have seen enough of them to have designed those surrealistic birthday cards. But what a joy it was to see the admirable Goldie voraciously devouring the animals' cake!

Yours sincerely,
Francis, Manchester

Celebrating Jack and Jill's birthday

DEAR BLUE PETER

I am very sorry to hear that Jill died earlier this week my sister grampa and granny and I grew very fond of her and are saddened by her dissapearance. Though she and Jack always did scamper away the cheeky things I know this will not get to the BBC on time for Thursdays edition. But I ask you to give her a proper sed send of. Maybe bury her in the garden a special piece for her. Once again we are very sad that she has gone and hope that she appreciates even though she is dead this little ~~cruel~~ present that I am giving her. Maybe you could get that friend of yours who made the statue of Petra to make one of Jill.

Yours sincerely

Deborah Williams

aged 11

P.S Could you possibly send me a badge and a reply.

Jack and (dead) Jill by Deborah, aged 11

1983

Dear Blue Peter,

I am very sorry that Jill died I think that she was a marvellous cat and made a good match for Jack. I was very fond of Jill.

Please please could I have a momento of her.

Yours sincerely,
Nicola, aged ten and eight days,
West Wickham, Kent

Dear Blue Peter,

I am very sorry to hear that Jill died earlier this week my sister grampa and granny and I grew very fond of her and are saddened by her dissapearance. Though she and Jack always did scamper away the cheeky things I know this will not get to the BBC on time for Thursdays edition. But will you give her a proper send off? Maybe bury her in the garden in a special place for her. Once again we are very sad that she has gone and hope that she appreciates even though she is dead this little present that I am giving her. Maybe you could get that friend of yours who made the statue of Petra to make one of Jill.

Yours sincerely,
Deborah, Clifton, 11

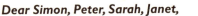

Dear Simon, Peter, Sarah, Janet,

We are very sad that Jill has died. I expect you are sad too. We have a cat called Floss and she has three kittens. They are three weeks old and we've named them Buttons, Podge and Tiger. If you would like one you could have one in three weeks and you can choose another name if you like. Two are grey and Tiger is a stripey tabby.

We also have two mice, two guinea pigs, a rabbit, seven sticklebacks and about 40 tadpoles. We did have six hens but the fox killed them.

From Toby aged 8, Lucy aged 7 and James aged 3½, Tamworth

Jack and Jill

Dear George,

I am writing on behalf of our two tortoises, Simon and William. They invite George to a 'tortoise tea,' and tremendously hope he can come. Any time after September 1st would be lovely, but not after October because Simon and William are planning to hibernate as usual again this year! Simon and William particularly like party tea and would like to know George's especially favourite food. (Simon and Williams simply love custard and blanc mange!) Simon and William can't wait to hear what it is like being a 'television tortoise', and would be extremely interested to hear George's life story. Lots of love from

SIMON & WILLIAM TORTOISE.

From: Emma Vallance

Dear Janet Simon and
peter I drew this picture
of Mr George Tortoise
from blue peter. I am glad
he's woken up I was
just thinking he had died.
I will miss Jack and
will you (pTo) get another cat?

Georges heart is pounding
because he is dreaming
of lettuce. And he is
hungry.
                Love David E. Matthias.
                        'Age 7

1983

Dear George and Blue Peter,

Our tortoise Turbo (aged 15) was a little bit worried to see George going to bed on Monday.

Turbo recommends 1 inch strips of newspaper preferably the Radio Times (it makes good reading!) for his bedding, as straw can hide unwanted nasties and be sharp on his face if he pokes his head out!

He also likes an even temperature of 45°F throughout the winter.

Happy hibernation from Turbo
Peter and Debbie, Richmond, Surrey

"I am writing to you with a small frog beside me. He is alive because he has been properly looked after. Please tell people how to do it."

1985

Dear Simon Groom,

I've got a complaint to make. If you knew more about cats you would know that you must never pick up a cat or kitten up by the scruff of the neck unless you are its mother, which I'm sure you are not. It hurts cats and kittens to be picked up by the scruff of the neck at that weight and age. I hope you don't do it again.

The rest of the programme was great. I'm not surprised it bit you. Peter's hair is best long.

Yours sincerely,
Joanne Orton, age 10,
Maldon, Essex

Dear Blue Peter,

I am writing to you with a small frog beside me. He is alive because he has been properly looked after. Please tell people how to do it.

I am ten years old.

John, London

1986

Dear Yvette, Caron, Mark & Biddy,

You must miss George a lot, so here's a marzipan George to ease the pain. Of course, you can eat it but we think it's far too lovely and sweet to put your teeth into! Hope you like it ...

Merry Xmas, happy New Year once again

Edith and Annemarie, Rotterdam

BLUE PETER

GEORGE

ⓑⓑⓒ tv

1986

Dear Sirs,

I wish to express my concern at hearing on "Blue Peter" that the dog GOLDIE has had 13 litters in 8 years – if my facts are right, I can only say I believe this dog is being exploited for gain. I would like to hear from you as otherwise I will write to the RSPCA.

As Goldie is famous it seems you people or whoever owns her, are cashing in on her fame – it seems totally inhuman and cruel that a dog should have 13 litters in 8 yrs.

I watch Blue Peter altho I am 51 – I was fed up to the back teeth with over-exposed viewing of Lucy (I believe this was presenter Duncan's baby) – why a very ordinary presenter's baby should be shown continuously night after night, as she was, soon after she was born, beats me – it got on my nerves.

I think all 3 presenters are extremely mediocre and boring to screaming point. I would like to hear about Goldie and what is being done to stop her being exploited – I wait to hear.

Miss Walker,
Leicestershire

1986
Dear Miss Walker,
Thank you for your letter of May 11th. You are quite wrong in the supposition that Goldie has had 13 litters. For a dog of her age, this would be quite impossible. Goldie has had two litters.

Your other comments have been noted.
Yours sincerely,
Biddy Baxter, Editor

I really think John's had enough!
Wee Shep is most terribly rough!
He nips poor John's ears
Till he's nearly in tears.
I'd cover them up with a muff!
Andrew Pender, age 8

1987
In these days of cruelty & violence to children, the elderly and animals it

was moving to see on TV a grown man weep for the death of his 14-year-old canine friend,
G. Palmer, Hove

1987
Dear Blue Peter Team,
I have just finished watching your Thursday edition in tears, as I heard of the very sad death of Shep. I've watched Blue Peter since I was a young girl. Now aged 23, and married with a young son of my own, plus pets, I still remember seeing Shep as a pup when he first appeared on the programme and ask if you would kindly show the clip again in a future programme as this would bring back many lovely memories for me which I may be able to share with my young son, who I am sure would love to see it.

Further condolenesies to John Noakes who has lost a very faithful if not always obedient friend.
With affectionate regards
Mrs. Pryor, Ealing

John Noakes with Shep

1

Dear Janet, carol and Mark

I would like to

tell you about the cat who lives next

door to me.

Her name is Ginny and she was

17 years old in February. She is a small
cat and very pretty. Ginny is a tortoise sbell
and white cat.

She is a homely cat. She likes to

drink running water. In the summer Daddy was
watering our garden with the hose and Ginny
liked to drink from the spray. Auntie says she
likes to sit in the bath and drink from
the tap.

When I talk to her she meiows

back to answer me.

2

I like Ginny very much.
I was 7 years old at christmas, I
like watching Blue peter every week,
I look out for willow.

love from Helen Forrest

age 7

1987

Dear Blue Peter Team,

My nine year old daughter Emma is distraught, her teacher and classmates at her School here in Stevenage are making her life a misery, she has been held up for ridicule over a poem she wrote about our tortoise being fed dog food. I am certain that it was your programme that gave us the information about preparing for hibernation! Our tortoise thrived on it. The teacher said it was ridiculous, she should have written about lettuce leaves. Emma is embarrassed and cries a lot. Please, have you a fact sheet stating that one does feed a tortoise on dog food? If she can show them, maybe they will not taunt her again. If you can help I shall be very grateful indeed.

Yours sincerely,
Mrs. Glover, Stevenage

1987

Dear Mrs. Glover,

Thank you for your letter of the 19th March.

We were so sorry to hear that your daughter, Emma, is being ridiculed at school over a poem she wrote about her tortoise eating dog food. Although tortoises are primarily vegetarian they'll benefit from some animal protein such as a little canned dog or cat food and we're enclosing leaflets which the PDSA and London Zoo have produced which mention this fact and prove conclusively that Emma is right and her teacher and school friends are wrong!

With best wishes to you and Emma from all of us on the programme.

Yours sincerely,
Biddy Baxter, Editor

1987

Dear Mark, Caron and Yvette,

As a student at Corpus Christi College Oxford I hold the hallowed position of College Tortoise Keeper. Unfortunately both this title and a long college and university tradition are in great danger.

During the summer term our college plays host to the 'Tortoise Ffair', an annual challenge match amongst the college tortoises and more importantly a fund-raising event for charity. However our last tortoise has been retired due to ill-health and because of new laws restricting the importation of tortoises we have been unable to replace him.

It is to you I appeal in this plight. I am writing to ask whether it would be possible for us to nominally adopt the Blue Peter tortoise, or failing this to ask your viewers if any would be willing to have their tortoise adopted by the college.

Finally on behalf of the College Junior Common Room I extend an invitation to the Blue Peter tortoise to visit the Tortoise Ffair in May and compete in the prestigious tortoise race.

Yours hopefully,
Vicki Vaughan

1987
Dear Mark,
I watch Blue Peter every time it's on. When I went to Stratford-upon-Avon to visit my gran she took my sister and me to the cat show and I saw Willow and I got his autograph. Have you got any pets of your own? I have got a dog called Shandy a goldfish and a hamster called Rambo. Did you know if a hamster is born as a girl it can change into a boy? Mine did. Have you any brothers or sisters? I have got a twin sister called Becky but she was born 7 minutes after me. Could I have your autograph please.
From Emma, age 10½, Falmouth

1988
Dear Ms Baxter
In this world of space & technology it seems that some things never change, like bathing the dog.

It was interesting to watch last Monday still the same plastic mats, still the same I-hope-the-dog-doesn't-run-off feeling.

What is this woman on about you may ask yourself?

Well! You had a dog washing session in July 1966, which my toddler Paul watched, then tried to bath his toy dog in the loo. I wrote to you about this at the time, you thought it very funny & sent a letter & photographs, which I have always treasured (copy enclosed).

In 1967 we moved to the market town of Clitheroe, the toddler is now at Liverpool University, not training to be a vet, but a medical student, who is doing very well & takes his finals next year.

I still watch Blue Peter whenever I can, who says it is only for kids?
Yours sincerely,
Mrs. Haigh

Bathing the dogs in 1966

1992

Dear Sir,

It made me very sad to read in the National Press, and to see on yesterday's Blue Peter programme, that Goldie the Golden Retriever had through age passed on. Her owner must miss her very much.

My interest is due to having one of her first pups, namely Prince, who has of course appeared on your programme a number of times. You will recall that he was trained as a guide dog and worked for John Bates of Guildford.

On his retirement, Prince was given to us by the Guide Dog Association at Wokingham, and we have had the pleasure & privilege of his company for nearly 3 years.

He is now 11½ years old, and is enjoying his retirement. I am sorry to bore you, but I couldn't resist writing to let you know about him, he is such a lovely dog.

Yours faithfully,
R.J. Parsons, Worthing

**Goldie's favourite pastime –
looking for goldfish in the pond in the Italian sunken garden**

Dear Blue Peter,

We have a West Highland terrier called Daisy. She always recognizes your theme music and she comes running to the television, and almost knocks it over in her excitement to see the animals. She likes all animal programmes, but we think she likes Blue Peter best of all.

Love Katie, Anna and James, Doncaster

PS A lick from Daisy to Goldie

To Mabel,
Happy birthday

M is for Mabel
a is for Angelic
b is for beautiful
e is for excellent
l is for loving

Have a great day

from Emma

TO Mabel

Hope you have had a
fantastic time at blue
peter in that 10 years
and hope you still like
being a famous Pet.

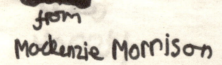

from
Mackenzie Morrison

Woof
Wooof!

Email 2002

I just happened to be flicking between channels, when you were skipping towards the end of your show. I was outraged to see that Mable was hurt and that when she went off limping all that was said was "aww poor mable" no one went after her!! This is terrible blue peter!

Dionne, 16

Don't worry Dionne I was just as worried when she launched herself into the skipping rope. She just can't resist trying to join in. Mabel actually got her leg caught between the ropes and was trying to free it. We gave her a dog chew and within seconds she was enjoying having her photo taken with the skippers. Please rest assured all our pets are thoroughly loved and spoilt by the presenters and a large production team!
Anne Dixon

BLUE PETER PEts
Lucy
Shelly
Mabel
SOCKS
Cookie
By Lara McGurk

Dear Blue Peter,

I think it was very very wrong of you to feed the dogs cheese on one of your shows. The poor animals. Would you like it if someone made you eat cheese on a tv program so you got lots of nightmares? I bet they didn't dare sleep after being fed cheese. It is a cruelty to animals to make them eat on tv weather it is cheese or not. They as animals also deserve there privacy.

Annoyed Animal Rights Campaigner

Don't feed cheese to dogs

Blue **Peter**   **Mabel**

Email 2004

I wrote to you lately about the presence of the cat on your programme. Surely you must have noticed how stressed the poor little thing was at the close of the Cat show today? It is SO WRONG for a dear little animal like that to be looked after in that manner.

Please talk to the RSPCA. I am sure they would totally agree with me. Dogs cope, cats don't. Please consider seriously what I am saying to you.
Mrs. Thomas

Dear Mrs. Thomas
Thank you for your email. There was an experienced cat handler present at all times during the filming at the Cat Show. Smudge is a five month old kitten who likes to get his own way. His miaowing indicated not that he was unhappy, but that he wanted to get down and have a look around, which was not appropriate in the situation. The majority of the time he does get his own way, and has a lovely big garden at home where he lives with Kari and Oke and Willow.

Thank you again for taking the trouble to contact us, and we would like to reassure you that Smudge is very well looked after.
Best wishes from all of us on the programme.

Email 2005

Could we have one of megs puppies because our died, she was 15
Ben, 10

Dear Ben,
I'm sorry to hear about your dog. You must be feeling very sad. I'm afraid we can't promise to give Meg's puppies away. Matt is keen that Meg's puppies become working dogs (the father is a working sheepdog). There are, however, many dogs just waiting for a good home (Mabel was a rescue dog) and if your family is thinking of welcoming

another dog into your home perhaps that is something that you could all look into? Meanwhile keep watching for the birth of Meg's pups!

With best wishes,

Richard Marson

Message Board 1st June 2005

Meg's puppies

I've got some great news for you all. Meg has had her puppies! Between 2pm and 8pm on Thursday 26th May, Meg gave birth to 5 pups, two boys and three girls. Meg is doing really well and getting to know them along with Ged, the proud dad. They were born with all their fur — four of the puppies are black and white and one is browny red and white. They have now almost doubled in size and are very noisy! We're deciding on names for all the new arrivals, so make sure you watch when we're back on air in July to find out how they are all doing.

Thanks for all of your good luck messages for Meg!

See you soon.

Matt

Message board responses:

Hia Matt! Give my love and warm wishes to Meg and all her five little puppies! I bet they're beautiful! *Lottsa love, Diamond girl*

Meg had her puppies on my birthday so I was wondering if you could call one of the girls Jo short for my name it would be grate because Ive never had anything of mine comp entries or anything I would be really happy if one of the boys were Bracken that's after my dog who had to be put down three days after Easter because he had cancer. *Doolally girl xxxxxx*

I think that one of the boys should be called Simon as a tribute to Simon Thomas' work on blue peter. You, simon, konnie and liz made the best team.

Shocked, Shepton Mallet

APART FROM COMMENTS that are gratuitously abusive, letters and emails of criticism are just as important to any programme as those of praise. They keep the production team's feet on the ground as well as proving you can never please all of your audience all of the time. This is especially true of a long-running series like *Blue Peter*, and during the past 50 years, successive editors and presenters have had their share of sometimes vitriolically furious correspondence. It amazed me how viewers – nearly always adults rather than children – provided their full names and addresses and I often wondered whether they would have been equally abusive face to face. In some rare cases where it was perfectly obvious that no reasoned explanation, for whatever our offence was supposed to be, would be accepted, I reluctantly resorted to a "Dear X, Your comments have been noted" acknowledgement.

We all strived for perfection and one of the advantages of transmitting "live" (until fairly recent times) was the extra adrenaline that pushed all of us, camera crew, sound, lighting, stage crew, make-up and wardrobe, floor managers, vision mixers – every single person in the studio – to give our best! There was never the second chance of a retake.

It is quite right for viewers not to make allowances when presenters make slip-ups but sometimes even the smallest error provoked an enraged reaction.

Peter Duncan's demonstration of Saucy Leeks in 1983 clearly tipped this viewer, from Shepton Mallet, over the edge!!

Biddy Baxter,
The Editor,
Blue Peter, B.B.C.1 Television,
Wood Lane, W12 7JR

                    Re --Monday 17th January 1983
                    Peter Duncan and Saucy Leeks.

         Surely the B.B.C. can afford the services of
a qualified home economist. If you wish to
demonstrate cookery you owe it to your young
fans to give them the best, i.e. a tested recipe
and the correct explanation of cookery terms.
I was shocked with the actual handling of the
grated cheese. Have you no spoon?

         Why spoil Blue Peter with an amateur
performance when there are many attractive
young people who have been trained to get it
right when it comes to teaching cookery
by T.V. presentation.

                    Shocked Shepton Mallet, O.A.P.

Five years later, when Roland Rat made a guest appearance as Peter's deputy cook, Mrs. Dear of Oxshott wrote:

Dear Biddy Baxter,

How can you ??!!! Maybe not you, but someone has allowed the odious Roland Rat to completely mar yesterday's edition of Blue Peter. I was watching the programme with my grandchildren & their friends & they were disgusted with the ungainly & ugly interruptions of the rodent. Apart from that incident, we think Blue Peter is quite one of the best programmes on TV – & the way the standard & interest are kept up is remarkable.

Yours sincerely,

Mrs. Dear

PS Please let the cat eat the rat!

Peter Duncan with Roland Rat as chef's assistant

1964

Dear Sir,

My daughter and I were viewing your programme on Monday afternoon, above date.

My daughter commented on Christopher Trace. He stroked Petra the dog, then mentioned about the dog's fur coming out. Just after stroking the dog he turned sideways, and started ladling some sort of curry out of a saucepan onto plates one of which he handed to Valerie Singleton. He put a spoonful of curry to his mouth and then spat something over his shoulder, was it a dog's hair?

All this without washing his hands!

My comment is please remember you must have millions of children viewing and we do try to impress hygiene on the children.

Yours sincerely
J. Lucking, Epsom

Older viewers – probably those who were hard of hearing – were vehemently anti-accent of any kind and also appalled by what they considered to be the presenters' lack of dress sense. Clothes often preoccupied them more than the actual content of the programme:

Dear Sir/Madam,

I watched "Blue Peter" on Monday for the first time in ages with my son and I was appalled at the dress of the presenters.

I don't mind casual clothes but when it comes to looking as if the dress was obtained at the local jumble – its too much.

I'm sure if the BBC are so hard up they cannot give an adequate dress allowance to the presenters – one of your "Bring & Buy" sales could help.

Thought telephone call to South Pole a waste of time & money & reminded me of the running gag Ken Dodd & Judith Chalmers used to have years ago on Radio.

Yours faithfully,
Mrs. Battersby, Hanwell

COMB REQUIRED
Bad General appearance
Join action girl Caron Keating in today's program
BBC1, 5.5 pm Blue Peter

Dear Sir,

Oh what a great yawn it was Blue Peter on Monday

1. Uninteresting subjects
2. Ruddy begging
3. Dogs & cats running wild
4. Ghastly Mark Curry. Goggle eyed.
5. Worst of all Caron Keating. What a sight
6. Comb badly wanted
7. General slapdash dress
8. Stockings looked like an escaped convict.

Who is responsible for this slap dash boring show?

Mr. Garner, Reading

1973

Dear Sir,

'Blue Peter' is the favourite programme of my family and my children find it not only fun to watch but very instructive. Today however my pleasure was spoiled when 'Val' wore a dress during the 'Roman Feast' which was not only unbecoming to a children's programme but downright indecent in exposing her breasts in an unnecessary manner.

It is a pity the very high standard of 'Blue Peter' should be lowered by such dress. Please do not spoil an otherwise terrific programme.

Yours faithfully,
Mrs. Dowse, Co. Tyrone, N. Ireland

Dear Biddy,

In the last 'Blue Peter' we were shown Peter Duncan bearing his buttocks in Japan, and next week we are apparently going to be shown Simon taking a bath. Is this to make up for the near legendary corset programme? (No wonder the show is called 'Blue' Peter). If so, is this because of the sex act 'Sex Descrimination Act'?

Yours
Alistair Lyons

P.S. If in future one of the presenters is going to strip off please sure that it is Sarah.

This was Val's *Blue Peter* Special Assignment – Brussels and the famous Mannekin-Pis statue. Dating from 1619 and 280mm high, the Mannekin-Pis is dressed every July 14th in a French army uniform – given to him in 1918 to celebrate the liberation of Brussels at the end of WWI. With it came the following citation: "He showed great calmness in the face of the enemy, & was aware of the need to set an example. For more than four years he maintained an attitude of supreme disdain for the occupying troops – and, as befits the oldest and most famous inhabitant of Brussels, he did his duty!"

1975

Dear Sir or Madam,

Will one of you please bye that Leslie a brassier, as she is to me a disgusting sight on a childrens programme, is she frustrated or is it for the TV men, as you should hear the remarks from my family, if a bra is too big tell her to try corn plasters.

Yours faithfully,
Mrs. Daniels, Kent

1979

Dear Sir,

I have often thought that "Blue Peter" was an extravagant user of BBC funds (the viewers money) BUT today's programme took the biscuit.

A "Blue Peter" team sent to Egypt! What a good idea! But for 7-8 mins of poor photography in fact a better film could have been found in the BBC files or better still supplied by "Hammer Films".

Mrs. Bonaccoris, East Kilbride
PS I have written to my local press

1979

Dear Blue Peter Team,

I am writing to you because my mum is cross with you for calling food (grub). Mum said a grub is a thing larva of insects or clearing ground. Please don't teach our young children slang. Use the right word. I am only 12 years old but I have 7 sisters and two brothers older so watch what you say.

Love from
Brian, Billericay, Essex

1981

Dear Madam,

At her own request I enclose a letter from my daughter:

"I think you have been very rude through the last three Mondays

and please stop it very soon. *From Gwen"*
It is not very detailed, as she is only 7 years old but perhaps it will serve to illustrate the disappointment we all feel at several items on Blue Peter recently particularly the programme about corsets, and about sulphur baths. Whilst there was nothing intrinsically wrong with either programme, it was a great pity that it portrayed trusted Blue Peter presenters in various stages of undress.

The programme seemed to forget that a great many children regard the Blue Peter presenters as trusted family friends, almost on the same footing as their school teachers, or minister. My children reacted with as much embarrassment as if their teacher had pirouetted in her underwear, or a neighbour had rushed through our sitting room with no clothes on.

Sadly, I shall now have to be as wary of inviting "Blue Peter" to share our Monday tea time as I am of so many other programmes.

Was it really the same producer? or was she away on holiday?
Yours faithfully,
Mrs. Hunter, Ratlo, Midlothian

Dear Mrs. Hunter,
Thank you for your letter of the 12 October.

I was sad to learn that you were disappointed with the recent editions of Blue Peter featuring the Symington Corset Collection and our Expedition to Japan.

The Victorian underwear with the regulation chemise, pantaloons and stockings could scarcely have been more decorous. The accepted modern day bathing dress is a hundred times more revealing.

I agree with you that eyebrows would be raised if a neighbour, teacher or minister rushed through the sitting room with no clothes on. But they would be raised even further if they witnessed Peter plunging into a mud bath fully dressed! Nothing would be more ridiculous.

Far from being prurient, these items were informative and presented with an innocence and freshness that has obviously delighted vast numbers of our viewers. Children have written to say that their mothers wore liberty bodices and their grannies wore corsets and many teenagers have asked for further details of the Exhibition Foundations of Fashion to help with their 'O' Level studies.

If it is any consolation your reaction is the exception, not the rule.

Blue Peter's only break is during the months of July and August, so the answer to your last question is no — I was not on holiday. I was producing the programmes just as I have done so for the last twenty years!

Yours sincerely,

Biddy Baxter, Editor

1982

To The Director, The BBC

I wrote to the producer of Blue Peter because:

1. They were advertising "Grange Hill".

2. They were telling us that they were going to teach my girls BELLY dancing. (My daughter of 14 thought I was being ridiculous & said that Sarah — on the Programme, Friday 19th, said — BALLET dancing!).

I know a HEADMISTRESS of a huge girls comprehensive — who thinks that "Grange Hill" definitely gives children ideas of WRONG DOING.

Also — I was having a normal telephone conversation with an elderly lady yesterday & she asked me if I had seen "Blue Peter" (22nd Mch) — she said she was shocked, "absolutely disgusted" — "it is one programme that has always been clean, decent, and exciting". She was "amazed" & thought it was "filthy".

Ever since Sarah and Peter came on the programme I have noticed a slight deterioration. Simon seems quite different — and more the kind of fine person we have looked for in Blue Peter. I don't know who is influencing Sarah & Peter and spoiling them! Sometimes like yesterday, I get the impression that someone is DELIBERATELY trying to corrupt our children (I know some of the Marxists do that sort of thing). Thank you for your attention.

Sincerely,

Mrs. Eeles, London

1982

Dear Editor,

If Peter Duncan wears that horrific suit again I shall never watch Blue peter again nor shall I recommend it to any of my friends.

Yours sincerely,

Mrs. Welthorpe, Newcastle upon Tyne

PS I'm just glad I don't own a colour television set!

Dear Blue Peter,

I warned you. Now you'll be sorry.

The moment I saw Peter in his garment again, I'm afraid I had to switch off. I hope you don't think this too unsporting in light of current events.

Yours,

Mrs. Welthorpe

Peter Duncan's suit was designed for him by a Blue Peter viewer

Dear Sir/madame

I watched your programe on Thursday 23rd December. This disgusted me when I saw Simon Groome milking a cow which produced beef sausages. Constantly this programe talks of animals and how much they love animals yet they do this. I am a vegeterian and I find this joke in poor taste.
Yours sincerly
Vanessa Rickwood

Dear Vanessa,

Thank you for your letter.

We were absolutely amazed by your comments about the pantomime animals you saw on Blue Peter on December 23rd. The tradition of sausages and other silly objects being "milked" out of the panto cow is one that goes back very many years. It's pure slapstick comedy and I'm afraid we don't agree with you that it's "disgusting"!

With best wishes from Simon, Sarah, Peter and all of us on the programme,

Yours sincerely,

(Biddy Baxter)
Editor, Blue Peter

1982

Dear Sarah,

Could you not do something about your hair? It lookes like hell all straight, skimpy, thin, uneven wisps! You have such a beautiful little face & lovely figure! Your hair spoils it all! One of my sons says he would like to take you out if you had had a perm – the older boy says he would like to but you would have to wear a hat!

Yrs R. Roberts, Colwyn Bay

1982

Young man,

You used the word "ain't" today in Blue Peter. As my old teacher used to say, "Aint – aint in the dictionary – Aint Aint"

Please remember the word should be – isn't or in full is not – or in your way of what you said – I am not.

Yours sincerely,
Mr. Carrington, Bedford

Simon Groom and Sarah Greene

"For Gods sake sit properly when you are wearing a Kilt. Pull yourself together."

Sirs,
Today Peter's pancake-fritter making was revolting. Give more time to this section or pass it over to Sarah. Such slovenliness in preparing a dish was one that no child should copy. The whole action was unforgivable. Fritters were either cooked black or under cooked and to offer our visitors these was a disgrace.

We have very competent children. So do not give them rubbish
Sincerely,
Mrs. Hollands, Worthing

1982
For Gods sake sit properly when you are wearing a Kilt. Not with your legs wide apart, even if your sporran is hanging down. Pull yourself together or come off the "Blue Peter" programme which you disgrace.
A Scot, Gloucestershire

1982
Dear 'Blue Peter',
I've enjoyed your programme enormously for many years and watch regularly with my 3 daughters aged 8, 5 and 3, who seem to enjoy the models, cooking and animals best!

Can I say however how upset and angry I was to realise that you seem to be having a regular cartoon spot! They seem to be irrelevant to the programme content and not even of a very high standard. Aren't there enough cartoons on childrens TV already?!! Particularly as Blue Peter is often followed by a short cartoon, it seemed totally out of character to your normally excellent programme. Please keep them out!! Otherwise best wishes from all our family & when can we see any of the presenters in Leeds?
Yours sincerely,
Hilary Brosh, Leeds

In fact *Bleep and Booster* was hugely popular!

Dear John, I watch your programme every week and find it very interesting. When are you going to bring back Bleep and Booster? Could you show more things for boys to mack. I thort the dols garden was very good.
Stuart, age 14, Brize Norton

**An original drawing for *Blue Peter*'s pre *Star Trek* space series –
Bleep and Booster – created by William Timyn and Dorothy Smith**

1982

Dear Sir/madam,

I am sitting here watching the latest edition of Blue Peter, and quite honestly I am shocked, horrified, and apauled. The three persons – Peter Duncan, Simon Groom and Sarah Green hosting the programme look like they have just come back from a refugee camp! I think it is apauling and it should be stopped immediately. There is no need for this gross indecency. They dress as if they haven't two pence between them! I have noticed the steady decline in the presentation of the programme since the exit of Val Singleton, Peter Purves and John Noakes.

Now come along this trio and look set to destroy the programme. It can only be a bad example to the kids that watch the programme. The three in question can dress casually without being scruffy. And if they are that hard up I would gladly send them a few bob to tidy themselves up! I wait in great hope that this letter will be an end to the scruff of the year show.

Yours hopefully,
P. Martin, Rustington, Sussex

Peter Duncan, Simon Groom and Sarah Greene with studio guest Kevin Keegan

1983

Dear Miss Baxter,

Having been a long and enthusiastic supporter of the work done by the programme 'Blue Peter', I would like to express my dismay at the use of the expression "Open your gob" used by Peter Duncan in last Thursday's programme. Surely he realises that many many pupils and youngsters accept the standards used on this programme as being the correct ones. "open your gob" is the worst kind of English for pupils to use or hear. I strongly deprecate its use on Blue Peter and hope you do too.

Yours sincerely,
Mr. Martin, Headmaster, Rudheath High School, Cheshire

1983

Blue Peter

I am disgusted to see on Thursday's 'Blue Peter' those females still in gear not in keeping with the programme they looked like a couple of tarts with those disgusting short clothes & those horrible long earrings, even my two children think they are horrible & when oh when is that stupid half dressed Sarah Greene going – you don't seem to want to part with her – well I can tell you lot there is a great number of people that will be glad to see her go so once again get rid of S G & dress that other one decently.

John

PS The film shown last week was unsuitable for children with bedroom scenes (please take note)

1985

To the Director General
Dear Sir,

A few years ago, on his first appearance on television, a weatherman included in his forecast the words "a wind off of the sea". We never saw him again. I suggest that we never see again the tall young man who, during the Blue Peter programme yesterday, said, "He is better looking than what I am".

Among the millions of unemployed can you really not find a young man with a pleasant personality, an adventurous spirit and some knowledge of the English language?

Yours truly,

Mrs. Crisp, Northumberland

1985

MR DUNCAN

REF YOUR BLUE PETER GETTING YOUR LOCKS TRIMMED, FOR GODS SAKE GROW UP AND ACT LIKE A MAN. BLOODY HAIR DOWN TO YOUR SHOULDERS MAKES YOU LOOK LIKE A BLOODY WOMAN. IN THE ARMY YOU WOULD BE MADE TO HAVE IT INCH ABOVE YOUR EARS & LOOK TIDY, YOU'RE A STUPID WOMAN. GROW UP FOR GODS SAKE, WHAT WRONG WITH SO CALLED MEN TODAY!

TV VIEWERS

Peter Duncan tries out new hair styles suggested by viewers

1987

Dear Miss Baxter,

Did my ears deceive me during today's Blue Peter or did I actually hear a dressed up Pig saying "Put your bum on a bike"? Please, please, please, we do not want to hear this sort of thing on your otherwise excellent programme.

I feel I'm fighting a loan, uphill battle to teach my children to be polite and speak reasonably well. Until now your programme was about the only one I could happily let them watch. Please don't force me to start censoring that too.

Yours sincerely,
Mrs. Alton, Harlow, Essex

Dear Madam,

My two children – teenage – want to know when you are going to get rid of Simon Groom and Janet Ellis. They describe them as 'dreary' and 'too pleased with themselves'. I must say I agree with them.

Why do all presenters of children's programmes have permanent silly grins on their faces?

Yours faithfully,
Mr. McCandlish, Mevagissey

Blue Peter, BBC London

Where does Caron Keeting get her rags from. The recent rags appeal or the local Oxfam shop? Is she practicing for the part of the scarecrow in "Over the Rainbow"? She is an utter disgrace to an otherwise decent programme. In our family she is called the girl who has come through a drainpipe backwards!! Get her cleaned up – PLEASE!

Dear Sirs,

Where on earth did you get the new presenter on Blue Peter. We cant understand her language, and I'm sure you mustn't pay her enough by the way she is dressed. She looks like nothing on earth. They don't need to worry about Anglo-Irish agreement they are all over here. What about giving the Welsh a chance. We are swamped with Irish.

Mrs. Lewis, Gwenedd

Dear Ms Baxter

Oh Biddy Biddy how could you let that awful Elton John video be shown on Blue Peter?? It was so anti all that Blue Peter stands for.

I've been a Blue Peter fan for many years. I'm nearly 60 but I still find it so refreshing. I've lived in India and Bangladesh on and off for 30 years & Blue Peter has been the one programme I've looked forward to watching. I shall keep on watching & will try to believe that the Elton John video slipped in by mistake. Blue Peter helps to put positive thinking into childrens minds & shows them there is plenty of good in the world. Please restore my faith that the 'Elton John video' was a mistake. God bless you all,

Sincerely,
Mrs. Skirrow, Chelmsford

Peter Duncan with Elton John

Dear Blue Peter,

I was very annoyed with your response to Burns Night on Monday twenty fifth of January. In Scotland this is taken very seriously and your behaviour annoyed all my family including me. It was insulting to the piper and also the butcher.
Yours faithfully,
Claire, Penicuik

BLUE PETER

Watching your programe makes me feel sick. As far as you are concerned Scotland is a part of England and the Union Jack is English. When anything is brought up to do with the rest of the home countries it is called British but when it is England it is refered to as English. Biased commentors who spout everything about England you would think England were the only ones in the World Cup all we have heard in the past months is how good they are and how there going to win. This is a load of crap for a team who could hardly qualify. As far as you are concerned we are a bunch of mindless cretons who wear kilts and shoot haggis. The only ones who wear kilts up here are stupid English turds who don't know any better. Anywhere Ive been in the world from Italy to America I find that people think the English are pompous and arrogant. Start treating us as equals or just piss off. England can stick their Union Jack.

This did not come from a mindless Scottish creton who has a kilt on
Mr. McKendrick, Glasgow
PS You wont have the guts to read this out on telley

Dear Blue Peter Team,

I feel that I must write a letter of complaint about the dialogue in the extract about the Natural History Museum. The Museum does not contain anything that nature has created, it contains things that GOD has created. Regardless of whether you believe the world as we know it came about by creation or evolution surely the true authorship of all things comes from God. I hope that you will take extreme care over the dialogue of further items in this vein, as we have not degenerated into an atheistic society. If you must talk about the theories why not show the other side of the coin too. Some scientist believe

that the world is much younger than is generally assumed so why not an item on this too. Remember you are talking about theories not proven facts. Apart from this the show is good.
Yours faithfully,
Miss Richards, West Glamorgan

To Janet, Simon and Michael,
I am writing to complain about the days you show Blue Peter. Thursdays are o.k, but I always miss Mondays as I am doing either gymnastics or ballet. A lot of my friends are out on Mondays too. I am a Junior Associate of the Royal Ballet School and will dance with Michael anytime.
Lots of
(P.S. A belated birthday to Janet)
Love
Jane Griffith,
(Age 10)

1987
Dear Sir,
As a child I used to always watch Blue Peter and now our three children view the program. I find it well-presented, informative and fun. I feel I can

safely leave my children watching it whilst I go about my evening chores.

Last night proved to be the exception however and we turned over to Blockbusters on channel 3. I do not wish my children to make witch puppets. In fact I do not allow them to have anything to do with Halloween. Why should they be involved in a festival that has its bases in the occult. The Bible (upon which our society is supposedly based) strongly condemns soothsayers, witches and so on. Halloween was originally celebrated with orgies and black mass (in which newborn infants were slaughtered). Please do not taint our children with this.

Yours faithfully,
Ms Walker, Crawley

1987

Dear Blue Peter & Biddy Baxter,
Until recently I have enjoyed Blue Peter, but now the programme is rubbish. Yvette Feilding is such a wally. Please, please can we have a more intelligent presenter. Her comments on the music room roof at Brighton were either pathetic jokes or stating the obvious!

Mark Curry makes me want to kick the screen. He's such a pillock, an idiot, a total wally; need I go on? Whatever happened to Sarah Greene when SANITY ruled Blue Peter. Come on get some some decent presenters.

Yours sincerely,
Peter, age 14, Essex

1988

Dear Blue Peter,
We enjoyed your programme on Burn's night, 25th January, but were horrified when you sat down to eat the Haggis and you didn't say the Selkirk Grace OR address the Haggis.

From Fiona (9) and Lindsay (11), Bothwell

"Mark Curry makes me want to kick the screen. He's such a pillock, an idiot, a total wally; need I go on?"

9th January 1988.

Blue Peter,
B.B.C.
London.

Dear Sir,

   I must protest about Blue Peter. The three persons
who present it, two girls and a man, their speaking voices
leave a lot to be desired, especially the girl from Northern
Ireland she gabbles away and one cannot understand a word
she says. She appeared a few days ago with a ridiculous hat
together with her shaggy mane of hair she looked like a
lioness enough to frighten a small child. For heavens sake
stick to the old standards of being well-spoken and articulate.

   I was weary last week of being pressurised to send
one more bags of rags which the three of them encouraged.
Sad to say in my opinion Blue Peter has deteriorated.

                    Yours faithfully.

                    Sheila A. Proho.

Caron Keating in costume for her
performance of Paddy McGinty's Goat

"Mark and Evette are always messing about together...Then they actually went and HUGGED each other. Are they in Love?"

1988
Dear Mr. Director
I have watched Blue Peter ever since I was five. I have always thought it was an interesting programme but now I don't think it is as good because Mark and Evette are always messing about together.

I have continued to watch for the last few weeks hoping things would improve but after tonights show I felt I had to write to you. Two things annoyed me on the same night! Mark said "is there a GOB around here". I don't think this is the correct language to use in front of young children. Then they actually went and HUGGED each other. This is somthing they do quite often. Are they in Love?
Yours faithfully,
Sarah, age 10, Manningtree, Essex

Email 2001
I was just wondering if you are going to start putting a certificate rating on your programme, my three year old son watches and this morning you featured a naked man getting in the bath which he commented on. I don't even allow him to see his own father naked. Blue Peter used to be a respectable programme, I will not longer be allowing my son to watch. Please reply.
F. Cavalli

Email 2001
I was eating my dinner when someone had put his whole arm up a cow's bottom!! I don't know about others but I did not find this suitable for tea time TV. I am disgusted at this. I do not believe it was real but it was still absolutely unacceptable. You call this education?
Thank you Blue Peter.

David Hughes
Email 2001
I am writing on behalf of my four year old sister, Julia who was terrified when on Friday's show when Matt fell into some quicksand. She thinks he is dead. I was shocked to see something so violent on Blue Peter which is a show intended for young children. I hope I shall never see anything like that again on Blue Peter.
Zoe, 9

2001
Dear Sirs,
I was watching the repeat of Blue Peter which was originally shown on 14th November 2001. I was very annoyed that you felt it was reasonable to show muslim religious practices and food on a childrens programme. This was done in light of the fact that many of the british armed forces are on two day alert to go and fight in a muslim country (Afghanistan).

The other main concern that I have is that we as British Christian people should be forced to respect the religion of immigrants whilst some areas of Britain have in fact banned Christmas lights so that we don't upset the muslims. My final question is who's country is this?
Yours Mr. Stock, Clacton-on Sea
PS My children have friends who's parents are in the armed forces.

Email 2002
Dear Blue Peter,
I noticed that on your "live" Christmas Eve episode the outdoor shots shown through the studio door showed it to be night time, but it was only lunchtime in reality????

Another one I noticed was Westlife made a tribute speech on 'This is your life' the other night from the BP studio, and today's programme two days later showed the band in the same studio setting. It couldn't have been a rehearsal because the set was identically decorated today, and I know you set up the studio at the start of the filming day.

Blue Peter used to be live everyday, and now it seems programmes are hastily pre-recorded and shown at 5pm supposedly 'live', but as you never advertise them as live anymore, it isn't certain whether they are or not.

Another giveaway is the v.v.v. annoying "coming up" captions you have with obvious pre-recorded STUDIO scenes being shown, not only conforming with the BBC trend now in blatantly ruining shows by telling us every intricate detail of what's 'coming up' or 'next episode' etc.

Please get back to the good old 'live' Blue Peters and stop ruining the MAGAZINE element of your MAGAZINE show – in other words let us be surprised with what's coming up! WHY ruin a perfect formula, BP worked for 42 years before 2000, why change it now? Stick to what you know best. Please consider these views,

Best wishes
B. Jones (15)

Sarah Greene, Mark Curry, Caron Keating, Yvette Fielding, Konnie Huq, Peter Duncan and Stuart Miles dressed for a Christmas Spectacular

Email 2002

I have been a Blue Peter fan since it first started, but I could not belive my ears today when I heard them talking about farting as my 5 year old son watched on. I know the BBC will always defend what ever they show and say because they are THE BBC!! But you'r not bloody parents, and I reseve the rights to what language my child hears, don't get me wrong, I'm not a prood I have a time and a place for my *****! But a five year old does not need to know the word fart! I've not used it in front of him so far, perhaps when he is 11/12 I thought. I'm really cheesed off with you lot, Biddy Baxter would'nt have let this one go on! You have betrayed 30 years of a English childrens insitiution. You aint got my view any more or my! Sons. What are you going to decide next for educating our childrens lingo; "Oh Simon, you made a right arse of that directing job" "matt you look a right tosser making that model" CHILDRENS TV! GET THE ****** MESSAGE!
Mr. Lawrence, 46

Email 2002

We have just for the first time in my life turned Blue Peter off due to the showing of eating insects, with chocolate. Sorry Chaps but this is not for children, and not at a common mealtime time
Vera and Thomas aged 7 & 5

Email 2002

Can I just say that I was disgusted by the sexual innuendo used in today's edition of Blue Peter.

After the making of a market stall one of the mail presenters said to the female presenter who had made the stall with Todd Carty "how much are your melons?" In a children's programme with such a good reputation – I was disgusted to hear such a sexist comment coming from one of the presenters. My daughters were shocked to hear a comment like this on a programme they normally enjoy and decided themselves to turn it off.
Mark Cunningham
(Disgusted parent)

Email 2002

I am absolutely disgusted with your show set in Morocco on Wednesday. You state that most people earn per day what we in Britain would pay for a cup of coffee, then go on to bargain with one of the shop owners. The shopkeeper would, quite rightly, like the full price for the goods, but instead Matt offers just over half of the price. The shopkeeper then kindly lowers his price but Matt is unwilling even to pay this. Matt gives the shopkeeper a choice: either except the lower price or he will spend nothing in the shop. Haven't any of the producers ever studied geography GCSE??? Poverty-stricken countries are being taken advantage of by tourists who barter for goods they can easily afford to pay the full price for and the locals lose out.
Ellen, age 15

Email 2002

Why are childrens programmes having stories about Spiderman the Movie when most of us cannot go and see it because it is a 12 film. It not very nice being told how it is then not allowed to see it.
Christopher, 8

Email 2002

I am horrified that you are now showing text messages on screen. Like many of your viewers my daughter is trying hard to spell correctly. Text language is very confusing for her and not appropriate for a programme that should be setting the standard for others.
Sarah Nicholson

Email 2003

Dear blue peter

I am writing to you after the program I watched today. I saw that one of your presenters was wearing an unsuitable item of clothing that was not appropriate for your viewers. I didn't think that it was advisable that Liz was wearing a top that incorporated the numbers "69". I think that this is very wrong as it was before 9 o'clock. I would like an official apology. You may not think that children of such a young age will acknowledge the meaning of 69 however I feel that they may remember this in the future and they could be scarred for life. After the show my 7 year old daughter asked for a top the same as Liz's and I was extreamly horrified!

Yours disgustedly Mrs. L.S. Hough

(Mother of a 3, 5 and 6 year old whom are all devoted watchers of your crude program, no longer!)

Dear Mrs. Hough
Thank you for your email.
The shirt Liz was wearing was a shirt with a number on it. Nothing more. We're quite sure that there was no intention to suggest anything by wearing the shirt and such an association wouldn't have been in the minds of our audience. We have a clear understanding of our audience and are very aware of our responsibilities. Many of us have children of our own with whom we watch the programme. With best wishes from all of us on Blue Peter.

Email 2003
Hi this is for the blue peter team. I saw this Fridays episode where Basil Brush was introduced and would like to know how many Fridays he is going to be on tv I ask this because he is so irritating and after the period of time I will be able to watch your Friday show again. He was annoying when my parents were children and still is!!
Amy, 14

Email 2004
I would like to let you know that following your program this morning, my 10 year old son is terrified of going to bed as he now believes that there are blood sucking bugs in his bed. He usually sleeps in just boxer shorts, but this evening he has put on a pair of long sleeved and long legged pyjamas

because he thinks the bugs that you mentioned on your program are going to attack and hurt him whilst he sleeps.

He has asked me on four separate occasions this evening when I last washed his bedding. To add to this fear, which has obviously been preying on his mind all day, he even asked whether he could sleep on the sofa tonight.

Could you please advise what you hoped to achieve by the content of your program as I'm sure that my son is not the only child to be behaving in this way since your programme.

Regards, Theresa Lawrence

Email 2004

Dear Blue Peter,

Yesterday afternoon I left my four year old daughter watching your program while I went to make the dinner. I was horrified when she called out "Mummy, what is a Gas chamber? Why did they set fire to all those people?" What on earth possessed you to feature this subject in such graphic detail on a prime time children's program. I realise that my daughter is young to watch the program, but the subject was inappropriate for any children's age group. It is a very upsetting subject which should only be covered in this depth by people able to mentally cope with the idea of such atrocities.

I am both shocked and disgusted and hope the content of this item has not left too many of your young viewers with nightmares!

Yours faithfully,
Stephanie Race

Email 2004

Dear Blue Peter

My sons and I have just watched a recording of yesterday's programme – 22/10.04, it focused on Konnie doing a Bollywood dance routine. I am disappointed that BP chose that particular routine as it was overtly sexual, what kind of message is it portraying to young people, especially young girls? Surely a less provocative scene could have been chosen?

Ms Currah

"The section on deep-fried tarantulas was FAR too detailed... and not for the faint-hearted and weak-stomached especially at TEA-TIME!!!"

Email 2005

Dear Blue Peter,

We watched last night's feature on Cambodia with great interest BUT... the section on deep-fried tarantulas was FAR too detailed and lengthy and definitely not for the faint-hearted and weak-stomached especially at TEA-TIME!!!

I am a confirmed arachnophobe who has always managed to keep my fear and loathing from my children, so I doggedly watched the item with them and kept quiet. I found that subsequently I couldn't eat anything all evening. Close ups of the frying spiders was revolting, watching the presenter gingerly trying one leg would have been more than sufficient, but to see him eating it all bit by bit was… uuggghhhh.

I would not have been happy to let my kids watch this alone. Would it have been okay to feature, say, monkey brains or dog being eaten in such detail??

Anne Forey

Email 2005

No offence but that stupid irish woman on blue peter with the stupid voice, what's her name, Zoe, is really annoying. We don't have a problem with irish people, my gran is irish so this isn't a racist issue. I realise you probably don't care but everyone in the class I teach is continually complaining about it and I said I'd do something as I agree. So please give her some kind of speech therapy. We have no idea what she is saying half of the time.

I like my students to feel they can express their opinions freely especially about something that is meant for them.

Thank you.

Mrs. Redmond, Plymouth

Blue Peter Babies

ACCORDING TO MEDIA watchers and analysts, one of the TV trends of the 1980s was role reversal. But it had all been happening on *Blue Peter* twenty years earlier! One of John Noakes's greatest triumphs had been his exploits as the programme's cook – far more entertaining than Valerie playing the chef's role. But the biggest role reversal of all was when the two lads from up north became babyminders. On September 30th 1968, Daniel Simon Scott made his first appearance on *Blue Peter,* aged eleven weeks. He was to take part in the programme for the next two years and John and Peter Purves were in charge.

Once again, *Blue Peter* was making television history. It was the first time a baby had made a regular appearance on TV and the first time a children's programme had followed the progress of a baby's development. It was an idea we had turned around for months, although there were enormous difficulties: would there be an avalanche of protests saying *Blue Peter* was being irresponsible and exploiting the baby? And where would we get the baby from, anyway? In the end, Sylvia Scott, mother of Bridget who had given us Jason, was expecting her eighth child. Sylvia was keen on the idea of showing children how babies grow up and develop and she certainly couldn't be described as an inexperienced mum exploited by an unscrupulous TV programme.

We decided to go ahead. Our only concession to caution was to pre-record the items on the mornings of the days they were transmitted. If for some reason or other Daniel wasn't in the mood, we would substitute something else – although this actually never happened. He became a firm favourite with the audience. Even a four-year-old viewer could feel "grown-up" compared with a baby. Lots of them wrote about their own baby brothers and sisters or that their mums were expecting a baby. And they were fascinated by the comparisons we were able to make with animal babies.

As the months passed, the studio items became more and more adventurous. There were visits to the swimming baths and to see the chimps at the zoo; a memorable chimps and babies' tea party in the *Blue Peter* garden and the making of a shed for the donkey given to Daniel as a first birthday present – with a magic moment when Daniel crashed a hammer very hard on John's thumb. We were never prosecuted for illegally bringing a baby into the studio and it was with great reluctance that we said goodbye to Daniel when he was two and a half. It would have been all too easy to have turned him into a male Shirley Temple. As it was, he would have no memory of ever being a TV star.

These letters are typical of Daniel's fan mail:

1969

Dear Blue Peter,

My favourite part of Blue Peter on Monday the 13th of January was the interesting discussion about the progress of a new born baby compared with a new born animal.

Val, John and Peter showed us Daniel as a very small baby. They also showed us Petra's babies when they were small. We were able to notice that the puppies were much more active than Daniel.

Puppies, kittens and all other young animals can walk after a few weeks but a human baby is about 1 year or more.

Jackie, aged 9

1969

Dear Blue Peter,

On Thursday 17th February I liked it best when John and Peter baked a cake for Daniel. They got the basin and put some butter and two eggs and some flour and when they had put all the things in the basin they got a clock and Peter said "Put it in the oven" meaning the cake but John put the clock in. Then Peter said "Where is the clock?" and John said "its in the oven" "Get it out". So he got it out and put the cake in the oven. Then Peter went out for a walk with Daniel and left John to finish the cake and when they came back it was finished.

Carole, aged 8

Dear Blue Peter,

The thing I like best about Blue Peter is that you don't just have only one thing. I liked your programme on Thursday February 27th because you had Daniel the baby & I have not got any brothers or sisters of my own and I have always wanted one so I like all babies or little children. There is a little girl next door who is mad on me. Sometimes I have to leave a note on our front door for her to take home to her Mummy to tell her what time I will come home.

Meryl, aged 8

Ten years later, a group of former *Blue Peter* viewers wrote to us from the Junior Common Room of St. Peter's College, Oxford:

1979

Dear Biddy and Blue Peter Team,

At the JCR meeting yesterday a motion was passed asking me to enquire as to the whereabouts and well being of Daniel, the Blue Peter Baby. It is now many years since Daniel has been seen on Blue Peter, and we would like to know what has happened to him, and where he is, what he is doing and how old he is now. As most of us were about 10 when he was last seen, we calculate that he must be between 10 and 12 now.

We would also like to invite Daniel to become an (honorary) member of the JCR.

Daniel, the *Blue Peter* baby,
on his second birthday

Please could you let me know about Daniel so that I can pass on the information to the very concerned JCR.

I'm looking forward to hearing from you in the near future

Yours faithfully,

Tim Eldridge, President

PS Why did Chris Wenner go to St. Catherines, not St. Peters?

In 1980 Tina Heath was the first *Blue Peter* presenter to become pregnant. She had met and married Dave Cooke, the musical director of the *Sunday Gang*, a programme she'd presented before joining *Blue Peter* and, after the Daniel experience, we decided the news would be of great interest to viewers and provide us with hours of fascinating new material. Having a baby brother or sister was very much part of the lives of our audi -ence and here was an opportunity to help many of them come to terms with their own mothers' pregnancies.

Every week there was some conversation about the baby growing inside Tina and children watched avidly as she got bigger and bigger. Being small and slim-hipped, there was little point in pretending it wasn't happening! The viewers responded in typical *Blue Peter* style. Cards and letters flowed into the office and with four months to go, Tina had 43 pairs of bootees, 99 matinee jackets, seven romper suits, 36 bibs, ten shawls and a luxurious rug of pure wool that came from the Orkneys. Her favourite letter came from a small boy who wrote: "I hope your baby is nice and sweet."

Joseph of Fareham wrote:

Dear Tina

If your baby dose get born on 10th september it will be the same date as my birthday.

From Joseph monk

By the time she was four months pregnant, viewers had sent Tina hundreds of cards and presents for her baby

Dear Tina,
I hope you enjoy having your baby with you and I'm sure you will enjoy it.
I'm terribly sorry that this is a short letter anyway
Give my love to your baby
love from Beverley

1979

Dear Tina,

I feel an explanation is required for the 'card' we are sending you. My 4½ yr old daughter was so delighted to hear your good news last Thurs. that she insisted on making this effort! We were so pleased with our son born last Dec., he is a super little chap & Rachel is a real help & thinks he is marvellous. She has drawn a picture of herself & Andrew.

Hope all goes well with you & we will look forward to hearing your news on Blue Peter. Are you going to attend the National Childbirth Trust classes? I found them so helpful & encouraging & enjoyed the birth of our two children, a wonderful experience.

Yours sincerely,
Mrs. Hawkins, Oxfordshire

Dr. Anne Cobbe, Tina's doctor, came to the studio to give Tina an antenatal examination. Tina bared her midriff and Dr. Cobbe listened with her stethoscope. She told viewers exactly how the baby was lying in the womb and how it would turn to present itself for birth. Then she showed a series of photographs charting the progress of the foetus from six weeks – the

"You will have Mrs. Mary Whitehouse after you, showing your tummy on television."

size of a tadpole – to four and a half months. When it was clearly recognisable as a baby, Dr. Cobbe produced an amplified stethoscope which broadcast the baby's heartbeats live from the womb.

The National Childbirth Trust wrote to me:

1980
Dear Madam,
May I congratulate you on the item about Tina's baby. You have done more for birth education in that sequence than we could do in years of talks.
Yours faithfully,
Sue Dale Tunnicliffe, The National Childbirth Trust

Dear Tina,
I have been watching Blue Peter as long as I can remember. I thought it was very interesting when they showed us your baby's heart beat and how the baby grows. Wishing you all the best in the future,
Yours sincerely,
Joanne, Cumbria

Dear Tina,
You will have Mrs. Mary Whitehouse after you, showing your tummy on television.
Yours faithfully,
Mr. Alderman, Tonbridge

Sir,
Surely it's time Tina Heath resigned from Blue Peter!!!! Having a baby is a family concern. Sex education is not for such a programme. Take the hint Tina – 3 presenters is enough,
Mrs. Jennings, Walsall

1980

Dear Sir or Madam,

Congratulations on yesterday's item and congratulations to Tina for her matter of fact approach to stripping off before the cameras. My 3½ year old was enraptured by the item (as were her parents!) I only wish you had put on the item earlier when we were expecting our second child as it would have explained points she found difficult to grasp (like the fact that there really was a live baby there!)

Yours faithfully,

Mrs. Rodgers, Rotherham

Tina Heath's GP gives her a prenatal examination in the studio. The baby's heartbeats were broadcast "live" from the womb

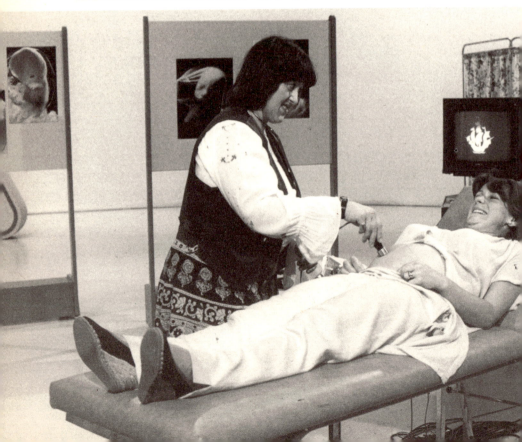

Dear Blue Peter,

I am utterly disgusted and appalled by Thursday 19 June programme. I thought Blue Peter was a programme for younger viewers, not EXPECTANT MOTHERS. I feel very strongly about that. You could loose a lot of viewers simply because of that. If you don't mind I would like to remain unidentified.

Yours, Miss S, Edinburgh

1980

Dear Tina,

My Mother & I (she is 97 & I am just on 71), so we are rather old children, like to watch Blue Peter, & today when you showed us a Blue Peter jersy someone had made for your baby, I thought you might like a pair of my special 'sock & shoe' booties. This is the only pattern my babes could not pull or kick off & it has never to my knowledge been printed. I had two pairs given me for my twin boys, by a very old friend of my Mother's and when I asked if I might have the pattern so I could make some more, she said she never had a pattern, only in her head. So I took one to pieces and copied it. The old lady has long since passed on, and I have adapted it from fine 2 ply wool which felted up when the babes sucked their toes, as babes will, to the more modern yarn that will stand machine washing and not shrink.

I sent the Queen a pair in 1947, & of course all my 5 grandchildren have worn them.

I hope you have a bonny baby & will be as happy with it as I was with each of my 5 (3 boys & 2 girls). Good luck dear

Yours sincerely,
Mrs. Stow, Ipswich

Dear Biddy Baxter,

I am a sit-down-with-my-cup-of-tea-and-watch-"Blue Peter"-viewer, but my son is an officer cadet at Sandhurst and he happened to 'phone me last evening – on Thursday 18th June that is.

I asked him, inter alia, whether he had seen the item on "Blue Peter" about the pace sticks wielded by the Sandhurst team. Indeed he had.

All the lads had seen it.

"Did you see the whole programme?" I asked, a horrid suspicion beginning to grow in my mind. He, catching my drift, assured me most earnestly that they had.

"Including the baby-bathing and X-ray session?" I enquired. "Very much including" he said.

I draw a veil (or perhaps a clean nappy) over the rest of the conversation, but I leave you, I trust, with a charming mental picture, in sound and vision, of the scenes within the sacred, all-male precincts of the Royal Military Academy, Sandhurst!

Yours sincerely,
Mr. Harris, Middlesex

Dear Biddy Baxter,
I feel that as a viewer of Blue Peter for many years I must write and tell you how much my two children and I (Paul 14 yrs & Victoria 10½) disliked having Tina Heath and her doctor carrying out her anti-natal examination on the programme. I also mentioned my views in the staff room at school (I am a kindergarten teacher) and found that several of my collegues who had watched the programme also felt that it was not necessary in a programme designed for young children.

Yours faithfully,
Mrs. Mallorie, Gloucestershire

Dear Blue Peter,
As a student Health Visitor currently involved in a series of health education talks in schools, I felt I must write and applaud you on yesterday's excellent programme. My eight year old daughter was enthralled by the ultrasound scan and sonicaid demonstration on Tina. Bathing the baby was also very well done too. Congratulations on a superb piece of health education! Good luck to Tina.

Yours sincerely,
Mrs. Bullas, South Humberside

Tina was marvellous throughout her pregnancy, never missing a programme and taking part in everything she was asked to do, including climbing a ladder on to the roof of Westminster Cathedral in her eighth month!

Jemma Victoria Cooke was born – with perfect timing – at one minute past three on a *Blue Peter* day, giving us plenty of time to prepare the announcement. Tina didn't want to return as a regular presenter but she brought Jemma to the studio on November 10th and made many more guest appearances over the years.

Dear Tina,

I am sending this bib for your baby. I hope you are well my brother Jonathan and I will miss you when you leave BLUE PETER to have your baby. I would be very pleased if you could send your autograph.
With lots of love from Annabel age 9 and Jonathan, age 6, Norwich

Dear Tina,

I am not very happy about you leaving because I will really miss you even though I am very happy about the baby. I wish you weren't leaving even though I know you must. Blue Peter will never be quite the same without you. I will wait patiently for you to come on with the baby. I am very glad Sarah came to help Simon and Chris. My mum and I really love watching the show.
Goodbye
Lisa Wilder

On Sunday November 3rd 1985, Peter Duncan's daughter Lucy became the third *Blue Peter* baby. Peter played a major part in her birth, as he cut the cord, washed her and put on her first nappy. Lucy was one of the youngest guests ever to appear on the programme when viewers saw her on film the following day.

Peter Duncan with Annie and baby Lucy the day she was born

It was a beaming Janet Ellis who told me in January 1987, "I want you to be the first to know – I'm pregnant!" She looked radiant and her joy was infectious. "So what's the plan?" I asked.

"The baby's due in the summer," said Janet, "so I'll be perfectly all right to carry on until the end of the season", which is exactly what she did. Her daughter, seven-year-old Sophie, was especially pleased. "She's in seventh heaven," said Janet. "She's been on at me for a baby brother or sister for years! We're spending next weekend with John's parents, to tell them. They'll be delighted, too." John had become Janet's partner after Janet's split and subsequent divorce from her husband Robin.

Janet told *Blue Peter* viewers about her baby in February. "Babies are in the news," she said. "There's soon going to be a brother or sister for Peter's Lucy and I'll be having a baby, too, in the summer." For children, many of whom were also expecting a baby brother or sister, this was good news:

Dear Janet,
CONGRATULAINS I would never of gessed. Me and my brother send our best wishes. I hope it will be a pretty little girl But Jeff wants it to be a boncey little boy.
All our love
Jeffery & Jocelyn, age 10 & 12, Romford
PS I have only been typing 1 month.

Dear Janet,
I hope your new baby brings a lot of joy to your family, and that you don't have to much trouble finding a name for it! I am sure it will have a very nice mother! Give my love to Bonnie!
Love Caroline, Surrey

1980
Dear Miss Ellis,
Although it is several years since I was entertained by your excellent programme, my two daughters are Blue Peter addicts. I was extremely surprised to return home from work last Monday (2nd Feb) to find my 4 year old, Katie, in floods of tears and apparently inconsolable.

By 6.30 my wife and I had calmed her to the point where we could ascertain the cause of her distress. Katie had been watching Blue Peter and told us that during the programme you had announced that you were to leave the series in order to become 'a mummy'.

I thought you would like to know that you have a great fan in Katie and wondered if perhaps you sent her a signed photograph – it would be a super surprise for her. Thank you for taking the time to read this and for an excellent programme – and congratulations!
Yours sincerely,
Mr. Whitehouse, Norwich

"Do you think I could come and help you to look after your new baby for a day and night?"

Dear Blue Peter

If Janet has to leave Because of her baby and we need a new presenter.
I think it would be a good idea for us to vote for candidates like an election.

from Nicholas Thompson
Age 10.

P.S. Philip Schiofield would be great

1987

Dear Janet

When I was watching Blue peter on Monday I heard you said that you were going to have a baby I love babies and I like looking after them very much. Unfortunately there are not any babies near us and all the ones that I knew have grown up. Do you think I could come and help you to look after your new baby for a day and night. When I grow up I would like a job looking after babies. I hope you are feeling well.

From Kathryn, age 9½, Dorchester

Wich ar
dar You
sunday havin
g
Mundy baby
Tuesday
medg
Thrist I go
frday
sauld

Genevieve
Cain
Age 4½

Translation:
Which day are you having your baby, Janet? Sunday, Monday etc!

Janet didn't actually begin to look pregnant for several months and she was so fit and healthy she carried on as normal, insisting on tackling quite strenuous filming. As far as we were concerned, the fact that Janet wasn't married to the father of her unborn baby was her business and hers alone.

But a chance meeting in March with a former fellow reporter from Janet's days as a journalist resulted in the news really hitting the headlines. The scandalous report was distorted and repeated in many papers and the resulting letters to the programme were a frightening example of how many people believe implicitly what they read in the papers. Some viewers rose to Janet's defence, like the married mother of two in Staines who wrote saying: "This is 1987 and unmarried mums are a fact of life. I have no fears that Miss Ellis's pregnancy will corrupt my children."

In July 1988 Janet had an idyllic wedding in a village in the South of France. Sophie was her bridesmaid and baby Jack gurgled contentedly in his granny's arms.

Liz Barker's son Dexter Todd was another winter baby. He was born on December 12th 2004, and Liz became the first *Blue Peter* mum to return to the programme. Dexter made several appearances before Liz left in 2006 and both he and Liz were sent many very affectionate letters and cards, but there were criticisms, too.

2005
Dear Blue Peter,
I am writing to express my disappointment in a particular feature on your programme, televised in February. Your presenter, Liz, had just had a baby called Dexter. Whilst it was interesting, with Liz at home with her new baby I found it inappropriate that she explained how she made up bottle feeds. I am a Neonatal/Paediatric Intensive Care Nurse and spend my day encouraging new Mums to Breast Feed their infants. The UK has the highest percentage of teenage mums in Europe, which is bad enough without children's television presenters advertising Bottle Feeding.

Dear Liz, it is sad
that you are leaving
I hope you have
enjoyed Most of your time
on Blue Peter from
Sophie Jackson

Sophie Jackson
aged 6

I felt this feature showed Bottle Feeding to be normal practice for a new Mum, when in fact Breast Feeding is normal & has been for a long time.

Sincerely,
Hayley Bird, Norwich

2005

To Liz

You're my best presenter on Blue Peter I will miss you so much I wish I can see you again on TV I think your baby is really cute Thank you for being a presenter on Blue peter Good luck in life and keep smiling!

Love from Fredha, 13, Manchester

Dear Liz

You are one of my favorot presenters. You've been great on blue peter. You where great on the bobsleding and lots of other challinges and weve injoyed you bieng on blue peter.

Lots of love from, Anna, age 6

LIZ

Sorry Liz that you are going
But it's time cos Dexter's growing
The time that you've been on Blue Peter
Nothing has ever beat ya

From riding bikes and dressing up
Making cakes and cuddle a pup
You are so great with lots of love
How will they replace you heavens above

We will miss you evermore
The time has come for five to be four
Even though we will be glum
It's time for you to be Dexter's mum

Good luck Liz
Sophie, aged 12, Cardiff

Liz Barker with Dexter Todd

2005

GOODBYE LIZ

I'm sad to see you leaving. I was sad when Simon left. If any more presenters leave I'll be lost. Hope you've had a great time on Blue Peter!

From Emma

The Famous Makes

JOURNALISTS REPORTING on *Blue Peter* for newspaper features were always hugely impressed by the daring of the presenters: John Noakes's five-mile-high freefall, Peter Duncan cleaning Big Ben without the aid of a safety harness, Simon's Tower Bridge Death Slide, Val calmly taking a fully grown lion on a shopping expedition, Lesley's hair-raising gallop on a runaway racehorse. That's how you get your audience on the edge of their seats, they'd say. And then gaze in disbelief when told that equal in popularity with the action films were the programme's "makes". The proof came not only in the enormous mailbags asking for the instruction leaflets and recipes we issued on request, but from the surveys sent in by schools all over the UK. Graphs and pie charts arrived in droves, from infants' classes upwards, dissecting *Blue Peter*. Voting for favourite items, presenters and pets obviously cheered up innumerable arithmetic lessons!

It seemed that no matter how ham-fisted they might eventually become, the creative urge of the pre-pubescent child was limitless. It rarely lasted into the mid-teenage years but the younger ones were total do-it-yourself addicts. Like Ben who sent this urgent request:

Dear Blue Peter,
Please, please, please don't make the Father Christmas Model on Thursday 16th December. I have to sing in the school carol Service and I shall miss it if you do. Mummy has bought the container too.
Love from Ben

POST CARD
THE ADDRESS TO BE WRITTEN ON THIS SIDE

Biddy Baxter,
Blue Peter
BBC Television Centre,
London W12 8QT.

In the early days, adult viewers sometimes sent in "make" suggestions:

1959
Dear Sir,
Just as the Children's hour programme was about to end last Thursday I heard someone saying – Don't forget to look in next week. I am showing a collection of dolls. I think the name of the announcer was Leila – my thoughts flew to my own collection and I thought you might like to show this one – It is made entirely of material starting with a piece of georgette for the face etc.

Would they please return it if it is of no value for showing.
Yours faithfully,
Frieda Ackerley, Essex

But nothing suitable arrived until one day in 1963, when a parcel came from Porchester addressed to Valerie Singleton. Inside was a collection of dolls' hats. They were exquisitely made and they came together with various stages and instructions showing how they could be made up from scratch, using odd bits of inexpensive materials. The sender, a mother of two small sons, signed herself Margaret Parnell. Valerie replied:

Dear Mrs. Parnell

We are all very thrilled with your two marvellous ideas for our programme and are certainly going to use them both. How very nice of you to go to all the trouble of sending them. We shall be making crepe paper hats in Blue Peter on the 10th June and will be using the ones you made us for demonstration. I hope you will be watching! We liked the ideas particularly, because they are simple, inexpensive and something children would have great fun making.

I am so glad you enjoy Blue Peter. We all have a good time doing it and try and find as much variety as possible. Nevertheless I am looking forward to next week when I shall be snatching some sun (I hope!) in France.

Again with very many thanks and if you have any more wonderful ideas do please let me know.

Yours sincerely,

Valerie (S)

This was the beginning of over 30 years of Margaret's brilliant *Blue Peter* "makes". It is not an exaggeration to describe her as a genius and it is a tribute to her imagination and skills that the makes became a favourite programme ingredient, loved equally by boys and girls of all ages.

Margaret's ideas have probably given more pleasure to more children than any other aspect of broadcasting since the invention of the cat's whisker. Her use of squeezy bottles, sticky backed plastic and toilet roll centres became part of British folklore and "Here's one I made earlier" has been lovingly parodied in *Monty Python* and *French and Saunders*.

Margaret never condescended to children. Her finished products, whether space puppets, draught excluders in the shape of dachshunds, punk outfits for teddy bears or cards for Mothering Sunday, all looked as though they'd come from Harrods or Hamleys. That was what impressed us most when she sent her first make to Val. Many other adults had offered ideas, but almost all were faintly tatty. Some of the samples had

Christopher Trace with a "do-it-yourself" egg box Dalek

obviously done the rounds of magazines and newspapers and looked grubby and dog-eared. Often they involved raw materials that were either expensive or difficult to get hold of. Margaret's makes always worked. The most clumsy five-year-old could come up with a reasonable end product – even if they improvised and used different materials. And Margaret's imaginative use of the nation's waste products was one of the earliest examples of helping the environment.

We ended up by scoring a treble. Children enjoyed watching the demonstrations, they enjoyed having a go themselves and we did more than our bit for conservation, making use of mountains of rubbish.

Valerie Singleton makes pencil case pigs out of squeezy bottles

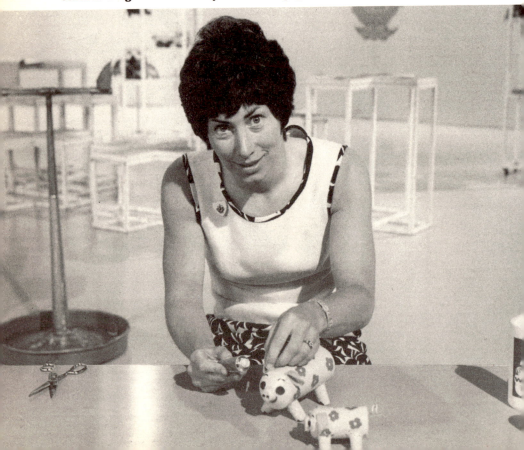

Margaret had never had any art college training – she had left school at fourteen – but she knew instinctively what would appeal to children's imaginations. Like us, she delighted in creating anti-commercials, making the accessories for Action Man, Sindy and My Little Pony for a fraction of the retail cost. These and similar toys appeal to children's strong acquisitive instincts, but often to the despair of single parents and the unemployed. One survey undertaken by *Blue Peter* in the 1970s showed it would cost nearly £1000 to buy all the accessories on sale for one heavily advertised doll. Margaret's ideas – like a ski-bob for Action Man, a caravan for My Little Pony, or her famous Tracy Island model – cost mere pence and included hours of play value. Some, like the Advent Crown made from wire coathangers and flameproof tinsel, could be used year after year. By the end of the 1980s, there were over 700 instruction leaflets available.

In 1984 an outfit for a teddy bear caused an uproar and the protests weren't all from adults:

What has happened to Blue Peter! Last week I was astonished to see an item on how to "Punk up your Teddy Bear". Apart from the fact the finished toy looked disgusting, children were advised to use aluminium ring pulls, metal paper fastners and chains to decorate the body. Viewers were also advised to "keep the toy away from younger members of the family". I think this was totally irresponsible and do not expect this from Blue Peter. What do you think?
Yours sincerely,
Giles (age 12), East Barnet

A grown-up viewer wrote:

Teddy bears should not be abused in such ways. They are supposed to be kind, friendly creatures – not rough & hard as the punk image implies.
Such a thing would never have happened when I was a child & watched Blue Peter regularly – in the good old days of Val, John & Peter!!

"Do parents really want their children to be taught Punkism/Punkery through their cuddly Teddies?"

Other indignant viewers wrote to Barry Took who was presenting *Points of View*:

Dear Barry,

In one of my infrequent looks at Blue Peter, I was horrified to see young viewers being shown how to transform their cuddly Teddy Bears into Punk bears, with full instructions about making Mohican hair do's, adding studs, chains, and earrings etc. Do parents really want their (sometimes very young) children to be taught Punkism/Punkery through their cuddly Teddies?

Yours sincerely,

Barbara Joy, Farnham, Surrey

PUNK TEDDY

Materials

Old black or white sock
Sewing thread
Brass paper fasteners and
  silver paint or
Foil and glue
Self-sticking material
  e.g. Velcro or
Snap fasteners
Black material for trousers
Odd lengths of chain
Wool (for hair)
Black elastic
Small rings or beads (for earrings)

The Television Centre switchboard took innumerable calls from adults "disgusted at the lowering of standards" in showing children how to turn teds into punk bears. But Ms Garcia of Streatham struck a blow for punks when she rang saying, "What gives you the right to take the 'piss' out of punks?" The television daily duty log noted a dozen more protests: "outrageous", "disgusting", "appalling", "sick", "in bad taste" were just a few of the loggable comments made.

Some of the makes had extraordinarily long lives. In 1993 Sue Hardy of Enfield wrote:

Dear Ms Baxter,

With all the Blue Peter Birthday celebrations going on I thought you would like to know that "something you made earlier" is still going strong 30 yrs later.

I refer to my Red Indian costume made, as suggested on Blue Peter, from a sack. My mother made it for me and I won first prize at a church fancy dress competition – aged 8. I still have the plastic silver cup which was my prize.

Over the years other prizes were won and it carried on doing excellent service throughout my teens, as several photos bear witness.

It saw the light of day again when, as a speech and language therapist, I learned the American hand signals… and ended up giving a demonstration to a cub pack; suitably attired in my Blue Peter dress. I also wore it one afternoon at work when all the staff dressed up for a party at the hospital where I worked – much to the amusement of our elderly clients! This year, as a middle-aged mum with a six year old son of my own, I found myself at a "Dodge City" weekend organised by the Camping and Caravan Club's Warwickshire District. The Red Indian outfit went with me, just in case, and, to my delight, I had an opportunity to learn real Indian dances with a group of enthusiasts who were part of the entertainment arranged for the weekend. How proud I was when their commentator paid tribute to the "authentic" costume I was wearing – as, apparently, squaws made their dresses from sacks and flour bags at one time. Little did he know!

Fortunately, the outfit was large and long when I first had it. I now wear it without the belt and it's still a decent length, as my husband's home video proves. I wondered if this is some sort of Blue Peter record so thought you may be interested to know about it.

Best wishes for the future,
Sue Hardy
PS Do I get a Blue Peter badge?!!!

Dear Sue,
Thank you so much for your letter of October 10th.

I remember that Red Indian costume quite vividly and am absolutely amazed that 30 years later it's still going strong. It must represent the best value for any 'make' there's ever been on Blue Peter, but what impresses me most is that 30 years later it still fits you! What a lot of pleasure it has given you and your family over the years.

Your letter reached me on the morning of Blue Peter's 35th birthday programme and I rang the office to see if there was room to mention it. Needless to say, the programme was full up but I am passing your letter on to my successor, Lewis Bronze, in case he can make use of it sometime in the future. I'm sure your 'make' must be a record and quite agree you deserve a Blue Peter badge. I'm also sending a copy of your letter to Margaret Parnell.

Thank you again for taking the trouble to write, With best wishes,
Yours sincerely,
Biddy Baxter

Amongst Margaret's ideas we occasionally included models suggested by enthusiasts that involved small propellers and electric motors. Jeremy Scott, aged eight, of Corsham gave this shopping list to his mother:

> ge t small m o t o r   and
> pa stick   bur peler
> matchboxs
> ~~Matchbox~~   plastiek 15 NOV 1972
> weorles   a nd   a   buwt
> ~~thas~~ ~~the~~ This   thick bolsore
> wood:
>
> 5 ~~teh~~ inctch   long .
> 3 inctch   a   cross
> the   vthe   way.
> This   thick .
>
> [rectangle drawing]
> wood

The modelling shop wrote to us enclosing Jeremy's list, with this *cri de coeur*:

1972

The Producer, Blue Peter

Nearly three years ago we wrote to you to draw attention to the impact your programme has on the local child population. This is with particular reference to the various models your team suggest the children attempt from time to time.

Since Monday all our three shops have completely sold out of a three months supply of propellors and wheels, and have sold some seventy small electric motors! This sounds as though we should be laughing all the way to the bank, but unfortunately it is not quite as simple as that as all our serious aeromodellers are unable to buy pretty basic supplies. In such a specialised field stocks can take ages to arrive – hence the reason for carrying three months stock. With a little bit of fore-thought this situation could have been avoided and many children would not have been so disappointed.

Dear Biddy Baxter,

I am writing on behalf of a child in my class, Wayne.

He is now 11, and since he has been in our school he has been a boon to every craft teacher. He has been a devoted follower of Blue Peter and has made everything you have made. We have never had anyone as keen on craft as Wayne. He is now about to go to comprehensive school. Is it possible for you to send him a Blue Peter badge? It would make him very happy. Hoping you can oblige,

Yours faithfully,

Mrs. Solie, Penywaun Junior School, Aberdare

Dear Wayne,

We have heard from your teacher, Mrs. Solie, how much help you have given to the craft teachers at School.

We're delighted to know that you're a great fan of Blue Peter and that you always try out the 'makes' we feature on the programme. Because you're such a great help in your craft lessons we're awarding you a Blue Peter badge which we hope you'll enjoy wearing!

We all wish you lots of luck when you start your new school in the autumn. With best wishes from all of us on the programme.

Yours sincerely,

Biddy Baxter, Editor

Dear Blue Peter,

I like your programme very much I enjoy watching it every Monday and Thursday. It is interesting I like the moidles you make I find them very good they are useful and I watch Vals special assignment too. My favourite city is Spain I like the bull fight too I watch it every Sunnday I like it so much I never mise it it is a good programme I am going to make moidleing cit and I like the dols house and the acshen man camp

Michelle, Bradwell Infants School, Great Yarmouth

Dear **BLUE**
PETER
I watch your program every week with my family. On BLUE PETER I think you have great ideas but, your best one was the christmas card with the stand out characters, I made 3 and they were all a success. Another good idea was the little hat, which was a pin cushion. Your last guy fawkes night was really brill and so is the program. I hope you have great success in the future. FROM CAROL FOWLES.

BLUE PETER

To Blue Peter
Please could I
have a Sheet
of how to make
a Pattern.
patio.

Love

from

Eva

Dear Eva,

Thank you for your letter and congratulations on your
excellent writing!

Here is the leaflet with instructions for a patio for
a dolls barbeque - we all hope you enjoy making it.
Because your writing was so good we are awarding you
a Blue Peter badge - it comes with a list of all the
places that give free entry to Blue Peter badge winners!

With best wishes from Mark, Caron, Yvette and all of
us on the programme.

Yours sincerely,

Dear Blue Peter
    We liked your christmas card idea
very much, and   we made some.
We also   used the   scraps!

                    Love from
                    Emily (9) Tom (7) Bethell

Happy
christmas
Blue Peter
Love From
Tom

My name is Jackie. I'm from America, New York. I'm over here on holiday, staying with mom & dad & aunt, uncle and cousins. I was sitting in front of the TV watching a nice girl called Evette (think!) making those personal organizers, and how they were so attractive. So I was wondering if you would be so kind as to send me the paper-clip design one that was terrific! Hey it's a shame they don't have Blue Peter in America, you make such nice things.
Yours sincerely,
Jackie, age 13

Yvette Fielding with all the ingredients for one of Margaret Parnell's "makes"

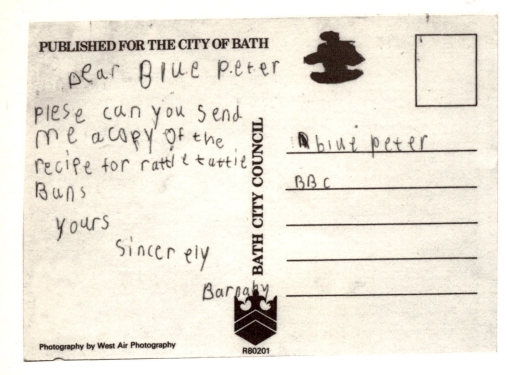

PUBLISHED FOR THE CITY OF BATH

Dear Blue Peter

plese can you send
me a copy of the
recipe for rattl e tattie
Buns

yours
sincerely

Barnaby

BATH CITY COUNCIL

bluE peter

BBC

Photography by West Air Photography

R80201

Dear Blue Peter

My name is Sya and I am eight and me and my brothers watch your programme when it is on. We like the things you make but we never have time to write them down so I am suggesting the idea of fact-sheets to tell how to make things.

My mum enjoys Blue Peter as she did when she was young but mums are so often making the tea at that time. I live on Lewis in the Outer Hebrides. I think you could make a very instresting film hear because people still speak Gaelic and weave cloth it is a very beautiful island.

I hope you read this letter and decide about fact-sheets.

Yours sincerely,

Sya

Dear Blue Peter,

I watch your show every week and I have always enjoyed it.

I liked those Christmas cards you made TINA, my mum thort they were lovely. The photo holders were good so were the boxes.

I wish you all a happy Christmas and a happy new year.

From Lynda, age 13

1999

Dear Blue Peter,

On Monday evening when Katy was cooking I noticed that she placed the pans on the stove with the handles hanging over the front of the cooker.

This is a very dangeorous thing to do and it is setting young cooks like my brother and I a bad example. Pan handles should always point towards the centre of the stove.

I think it would be a good idea if you reminded viewers of this very important safety issue.

Yours sincerely,

James and Thomas, ages 8 & 11, Tadcaster

Dear Biddy,

As a mum of 41 with children who grew up with Blue Peter & who grew up with it herself – please don't change. I heard you talk on Radio 4 and agree whole heartedly with what you said.

Please let young children continue to watch & do makes. The garden is marvellous and pets wonderfull. My boys are 14 & 11 and still enjoy watching. As you say, drugs & sex are catered for on other childrens programmes. As mothers we know we can sit young children down without worry to watch Blue Peter.

Keep up the good work – don't change for change sake.

Yours sincerely

Mrs. Fenn

In 1993 Anthea Turner showed how to make what can only be described as Margaret's *pièce de resistance*!

Her model of Tracy Island from the hit series *Thunderbirds* caused a deluge of requests for the instruction leaflet. Every member of the production team as well as the entire Correspondence Unit had to take leaflets home with them, spending evenings stuffing them into envelopes, in order not to disappoint the thousands of children who asked for them.

Cilla Collar, who was Head of the Correspondence Unit at that time, remembers it vividly, and estimates that 150,000 leaflets were posted.

In 2000, when a film was made of the series, it was *Thunderbirds* fever all over again. This time it was Konnie who made Tracy Island and once again there was a huge demand for the instructions.

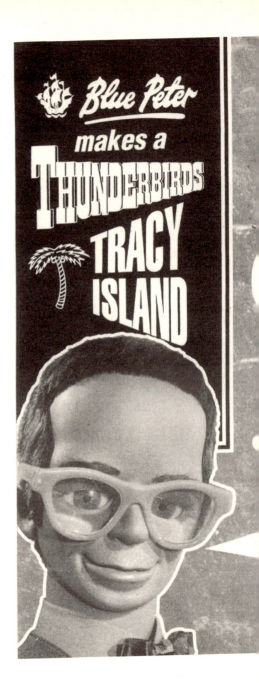

MATERIALS

Grocery carton. Cereal packet cardboard. Newspaper. Kitchen foil. Flour. Oblong tissue box. Oblong cheese box. Paper plate. Large yoghurt tub. Kitchen roll tube. Rubber solution glue. ll self-adhesive labels. Black pen. 3"/75mm. flowerpot saucer. Sandpaper. 2 medium and 1 small matchboxes. Sponge. Drinking straw. Scrap of polystyrene tile or packing. Corrugated paper. Brass paper fastener. Pipe cleaners. Green, brown and blue paper. Matt paint in green, brown and dark grey. Emulsion paint in white and pale grey.

In March 2008 Megan of Wisbech emailed the programme:

Hello,
I have been sorting out some old cards and letters of an elderly uncle and have come across handmade Christmas cards from 1965-1975 which were sent to him and which state they are Blue Peter design. There are 6 in all. Are you interested in seeing them and would you like me to post them to you? Loved the show when the children were small.
Best wishes,
Megan

What a tribute to Margaret Parnell that these cards were treasured and survived for 41 years – even longer than her Red Indian costume!

Andy Akinwolere demonstrates some more recent Margaret Parnell Christmas card designs

The Appeals

"WHICH WAS THE best of the *Blue Peter* Appeals?" is a question I'm often asked – but never answer, for it would be invidious to single one out. It would also be contrary to the whole spirit of the Appeals – the aim has never been to raise the maximum amount of money but to allow the maximum number of viewers to take part. This is why we never asked for cash and why we decided to collect rubbish, with a reclamation value, that the very poorest child would be able to find, and why our targets were worked out in multiples of rubbish that could be sent by the cheapest post. The cost of taking part was no more than the price of a second class stamp. And when the Bring and Buy Sales were launched – an inspired idea of Edward's – the bringers played an equally important part as the buyers. Because the size of the audience was so vast, every little bit really did help and no child was excluded.

We also had the advantage of being able to show not only the need of whichever good cause was being supported, in vivid visual terms, but also the impact of the Appeal results – and, just as important, the follow-up.

We were able to point out the often forgotten need for continuing responsibility with appeals such as lifeboats and Guide Dogs for the Blind. And although the appeals themselves were enormously varied, one thing remained the same: the launch date was always in the weeks before Christmas – and for a very good reason: prior to 1962, a Christmas display of toys had been a regular feature on *Blue Peter*. Edward, Rosemary and I thought that giving such a gigantic boost to the toy trade was unfair to poorer families who couldn't possibly afford these expensive items. At the same time, mouth-watering toy advertisements on Independent Television during children's programmes were increasing the "what am I going to get?" frenzy. So with only three days notice, we cancelled the display – leaving a large hole in the programme. "You said you were worried about the children who couldn't afford toys," Edward said, "so can't we find a way of asking the better-off children to give their old toys to people who aren't going to get anything for Christmas?" It was out of this conversation that the *Blue Peter* Appeals were born. Three days later, at the beginning of December 1962, Chris and Val announced the first Appeal. It was extremely simple.

"There are thousands of children who have nothing and thousands more who have very, very little for Christmas. If you are one of the lucky ones, see if you can find a toy to send to someone who's not so lucky. And we don't mean something that's dirty, tatty and broken." Chris held up a very grizzled teddy bear with one arm and chucked it away. "Send us something that will give someone as much pleasure as that something gave you when it was new. And send it to the *Blue Peter* Appeal…"

This was the first time those words were spoken on television. The response to that first Appeal was amazing and terrifying. We had no depot, no labour, no charity to run the Appeal. Just us and mountains and mountains of parcels. We learned a lot. But, most of all, we learned that if you ask *Blue Peter* viewers to do something, they never do it by halves!

The following year we ran the same Appeal and had the same tremendous response. We got in touch with our friends in the RAF who had flown the helicopter that had released thousands of balloons when we'd launched the *Blue Peter* badge. This time we organised helicopter drops on orphanages to deliver great sacks of toys on Christmas Eve.

In the autumn of 1964, a friend asked me if I had any silver paper. "It's for the Guide Dogs for the Blind," she said. And that was the beginning of *Blue Peter's* 44-year association with Guide Dogs. We appealed for silver paper, which had a high scrap value, to buy and train one guide dog for the blind, which cost £250 – a considerable sum in those days. This time we enlisted the help of the 8th St. Marylebone Scout Troop. We filmed at the scouts' hall where all the parcels were unpacked, and on the first programme after Christmas, Val and Chris triumphantly bowled a huge ball of silver paper round the studio. We'd done it! "You've sent us enough silver paper not just for one but two and a half guide dogs," announced Chris. And then we had a year following the puppy-walking and training of Honey, the programme's very first guide dog.

The Appeals became a regular, eagerly anticipated annual event and they caught the imagination of the country at large. The 1967 Appeal for stamps to help the homeless, in particular, seemed to affect everyone in Britain. Mandrake in the *Daily Telegraph* said: "When I saw my colleagues who ought to have been in the pub solemnly going through the waste paper baskets cutting stamps off all the envelopes I knew this was going to be big. Every home in Britain seems to be full of envelopes with the top right-hand corner ripped off, and that apparently includes the big house at the end of the Mall." The adults were caught up in the drive that started with their children.

Right from the start, we were determined that charity did not only belong at home. The UK-based Appeals alternated with those for good causes abroad, to the distaste of some adult viewers, but very rarely children. We never pulled our punches with the Appeals; no attempts were made to sanitise the horrors of civil war, famine, drought or disability, but children were never left without hope. Through their efforts lives could be transformed. In 1968, when we asked for old wool and cotton to help children who were the victims of the Nigerian/Biafran Civil War, we showed film of children and babies in advanced stages of *kwashiorkor,* with

In 1964 viewers were asked to collect 3 tons of silver paper and foil to provide a guide dog for the blind. The result was 7 tons obscenely distended stomachs, skeletal arms and legs and hollow eyes. They were in desperate need of the medical aid that was our target.

A mother wrote to say:

> My little boy is 4½. He has been to the neighbours and collected five socks and three pillowcases and we have just been to the post office to send the parcel. He is now firmly convinced that all the babies are better – there is no more sickness or famine.
>
> I am sure you will agree that he is a little young to be disillusioned, but I want to thank you for showing my son who has a roof over his head, enough to eat and a loving home that some children and babies are not so fortunate.

Three outstanding benefactors of the Appeals have been the haulage firm Roadline (later part of Lynx Parcel Force), the Post Office and the auctioneers, Phillips of Bond Street. In the 1970s shop stewards at Roadline suggested to their management that free delivery should be granted for all *Blue Peter* Appeal parcels. In a similar spirit, ever since 1972, following the Treasure Hunt Appeal, Phillips of Bond Street have organised sales of the many collectors' items donated, charging no commission. In 1972 the Treasure Hunt sale alone raised £6,159. In 1982 the first sale of collectors' items raised £77,800! And in 1984 Sir Ron Dearing, Chairman of the Post Office, offered Freepost delivery of all Double Lifesaver Appeal letters and parcels.

Overwhelmingly, the common denominator of all the Appeals has been the enthusiasm and generosity of viewers, from the youngest to the oldest, to do their utmost to help those in need. Occasionally, the "joining-in" is taken to extremes – like the time we were appealing for old toy cars and electrical plugs for a fleet of buses to take elderly, housebound people to day centres and clubs. A letter arrived, saying, "If you receive this parcel, please don't tell us on *Blue Peter*, we've sent you the plug from our set."

In 1971 this letter gave our Appeal to provide a dormitory for the

Starehe Boys Centre in Kenya a most welcome boost. Our target that year was 3,000,000 parcels of old wool and cotton.

Dear Sir,

We would like to help with your appeal for wool and cotton, so at our meeting today the staff of BRSPL [British Road Services Parcels Ltd] have agreed to collect and deliver all parcels marked Blue Peter without collecting any bonus for these parcels, thus cutting the postage cost – for instance a parcel 26lb 8oz from Fife to your London depot would be 50p with a next day delivery. Of course smaller parcels would be a lot less. We have the full backing of the Transport and General Workers Union for this project so if any of your viewers has a parcel please tell them to bring it along to their nearest depot or phone the depot to arrange a collection at no extra cost. Please mention Blue Peter when calling or phoneing.
P. Haines, Drivers Room, Acton, London

Princess Anne and Valerie Singleton at Nairobi's Starehe Boys' School Rescue Centre. *Blue Peter* viewers provided two new dormitories for the school in 1972

1973

Dear Val, John and Peter,

Our Dad thought that you would like to see these two photographs of a 'Blue Peter' tractor. It is working on a farm belonging to a school near Jinja, called Wairaka where the pupils can learn how to make their own farms grow more food. Most of the farms in Uganda are small, sometimes only 1 or 2 acres. They are called shambas. Because they are small not many farmers can afford their own tractor so they have co-operatives where they can hire tractors from. Our Dad teaches at another school nearby where they also have a farm. Even though most of the farms are small, farming is very important in Uganda because a lot of Ugandan exports like cotton, coffee and tea are grown on these small farms.

Although we expect it is very cold in England now, it is still very hot out here. We miss seeing Blue Peter and other programmes like Tom and Jerry, but it is very nice to be able to play out in the garden in January.

Ian, Karen and Stuart, Jinja, Uganda

1973

Dear Val, John, Peter and Lesley,

I am staying in my caravan at North Berwick and today something very exciting happened which I thought you may like to hear about. The new

Blue Peter inshore rescue boat arrived here 10 days ago and this morning it went into the sea to rescue a boy who was sixteen. He had floated out to sea a long way on an airbed and could not get back. This was the first time it had been in the sea. In the afternoon the crew were practicing in it. The skipper said that they were running the engine in. He is very pleased to have it in North Berwick because it rescued people so much quicker and much cheaper than big life boats. He was very grateful to all the Blue Peter viewers who helped to buy it – the only one in Scotland he said.

From Alison, age 8, York

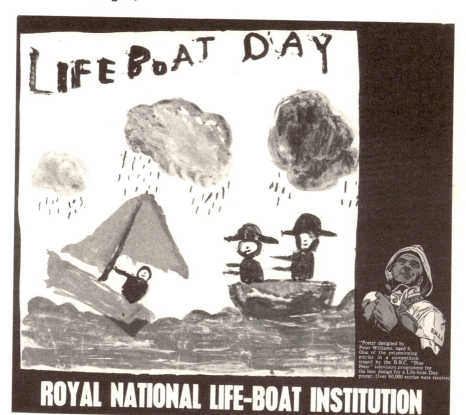

Poster designed by Peter Williams, aged 6, one of the top prizewinning entries in the Blue Peter competition to design a Lifeboat Day poster

1974

Sir,

I am writing to you to say a very big thank you for the very best holiday I think I have had. I also met some Salvation Army friends that I had not seen for 33 years & what a time we spent together. You see if there was no kind people like you to help people like me & others I should not perhaps seen my friends perhaps again & all because you made it possible & what a wonderful holiday I cannot put words together to thank you.

Lots of love & best of wishes from a very greatfull senior citizen as I shall be 90 next Xmas day. I do hope you will accept of my greatfull thanks & thank you again. God Bless you!

from Mrs. A. Hasters, Blue Peter Holiday Centre, Sandown

1974

Dear J L & P

Congratulations on the success of your BBBs appeal. A wonderful achievement. May I suggest that you think up a scheme to pull the BBC out of the Red. I am sure you can do it.

Yours sincerely,
OAP viewer, Staffordshire

1976

Dear Blue Peter,

While on holiday in Dorset with my parents we visited Forde Abbey. In the car park was one of the Blue Peter Old People's Buses.

This was the first thing bought by Blue Peter that I had seen. It was very nice to see something which I had contributed to.

Yours sincerely,
Jo, Kendal

1976

THANK you 'Blue Peter' for an enjoyable afternoon & evening. Preparing these stamps for your appeal has made this useless OAP feel she can still contribute in some small way to help others worse off than herself.

Dear Blue Peter,
I have just been watching your program and I saw the film about Beirut & heard about the stamps you want. These are all the stamps I could find now, but as soon as I have more, I will send them to you. I am an 18 year old Lebanese and I am very grateful to you for wanting to help us in Lebanon. The war has ruined thousands and many people are in need of help urgently. If there is anything I can do to help my people at home please let me know.
Thank you for all you do for Lebanon.
Diana, London

Viewers sent over six million envelopes of stamps for the 1973 Appeal for the Ethiopian drought and famine. In 1976 stamps were collected again for the Lifeline-Lebanon Appeal

"A few lads and me was wondering if you have a few of your badges which you could send us."

1977

Dear Sir,

The enclosed letter has been written by one of our trainees. I can confirm that the boys have been collecting their stamps for your appeal for a number of weeks. In view of the circumstances in which these young men find themselves I would be grateful if their request receives no open publicity.

Yours sincerely,

M. Kealey, Principal Officer, HM Borstal Hewell Grange

Dear Sir,

We, here at the Hewell Grange have been collecting stamps for you. We were told that you needed about six million to help some missionaries. It was a member of the public from a nearby village that told us as we are unable to watch the TV due to the hours we work. We have been collecting stamps and sending them to you for some weeks now.

A few of the lads and me was wondering if you have a few of your badges which you could send us. So all the lads at Hewell Grange wish you all the best of luck with your appeal and all your future appeals.

Yours truly,

The lads from Hewell Grange

1977

Dear Sirs,

I write to tell you that I have today sent off a parcel of 600 stamps collected by the prisoners on my wing for the Lifeline Lebanon appeal. Busy as I am sure you are I would if I could ask you to send a brief 'thank you' note. That sort of thing means very much to a man serving a lengthy term of imprisonment as almost all here are.

If you address the note c/o me I shall display it on the wing notice board.

Yours faithfully,

Peter M. Quinn, Assistant Governor, HM Prison Long Lartin

1977

Dear Everyone,

We have received your donation towards our Blue Peter Lifeline Lebanon Appeal to extend the stay of the British medical teams giving help to the sick and injured babies and children who are victims of the Civil War.

We do appreciate your generosity. Thanks to you and other Blue Peter viewers, these children will receive proper care and treatment that would otherwise have been denied to them. We thought you might like to have this specially autographed photograph of the Blue Peter team for your wing notice board.

With best wishes from all of us on the programme,
Yours sincerely,
Biddy Baxter, Editor

1977

Dear Biddy Baxter,

The children from our school have collected postage stamps for your appeal this year which I have sent off to the depot.

In fact your appeal has had a special meaning for us this year as four of our youngsters could have been among the casualties in the Lebanon. Beirut was their home but they were lucky enough to be in a position to move out when hostilities started. One boy, who was born in Beirut, has had a terrible feeling of guilt even since he has been with us – he feels that they should have stayed in Beirut to fight. He feels that they have betrayed their friends and fellows and for a year or so would write pages of essays on the subject – and he is only twelve now.

With all good wishes to you and all the Blue peter team, I am
Yours sincerely,
Mrs. Keating, Millfield Junior School

1979

Dear Miss Baxter,

A few months ago you were kind enough to write to me on behalf of my son Ian. He cannot read or write, is an epileptic and is psychologically unstable. At the age of 25, he is getting worse, He is an ardent Blue Peter fan & has for all your appeals sent a contribution. This year at the jeweller where I work we have saved him all our stamps from our parcels. Also my employer's wife who is South African has saved him stamps from relatives letters which I have enclosed.

Two days before Christmas I brought Ian the last of the stamps. Expecting him to be delighted instead he burst into tears, then got into one of his states, which took all my lunch hour to pacify him, get him calm enough to talk too, and to take his Valium and eat something. Some thoughtless person had told him he was wasting his time collecting stamps for Blue Peter as they should help our own people. Ian was beside himself, he sobbed, screamed at me Blue Peter are good people, they do kind things for everyone. I am helping aren't I. Tell me the truth. However here are Ian's stamps. If you could just spare time to write a little note to him telling him he has helped I would be so greatful. I realize you cannot thank everyone. If you could just let Ian know that his effort is not in vain then if next time anything is said to him he can say Blue Peter has told me they are pleased with my stamps and I am helping. I know you are busy but if you could just reassure Ian that he matters in this world. You will have made him very happy and helped me because I told him Blue Peter would be pleased with what he sent.
Yours sincerly,
M.G. Caulton – Ian's mum

1979

Dear Ian,
Thank you very much for your marvellous donation of stamps for our Medi-Bike Appeal. Although we have already reached our Target of 400 bikes, the need for them is so great, we are trying to get as many more as possible, and are keeping our Depot open until the end of March.

We thought you might like to know just how your stamps will help. This year has been made The International Year of the Child by the Untied Nations. The idea is to do everything possible for the millions of children in the world, specially those who suffer because of poverty. All the stamps and coins that are collected will be used to buy special bikes, with Medical Kits which will be sent to Tanzania. The Bikes will be used by Health Workers to visit remote villages speedily and give medical help to expectant mothers, babies and small children.

We are very grateful for all your help. We thought you might like to have this Blue Peter Emblem and this photograph which Lesley, Simon and Christopher have autographed specially for you.

With best wishes from Lesley, Simon, Christopher and all of us on the programme.

Yours sincerely,

Biddy Baxter, Editor

Dear Blue peter

I think it is bad that you did not tell us to cut carefully around the stamps

from Saffron McCullagh. (Age 5)

In 1979 the *Blue Peter* Appeal for Cambodia was the most successful in the history of the programme. The news of Pol Pot's disgusting acts of genocide shocked the world and that summer nearly all the letters in the *Blue Peter* postbag were saying one thing – could we do something to help the disaster that has happened in Cambodia? The fact that two million people had died and another three million were likely to starve to death by Christmas meant we had to act fast. There was no time to collect rubbish and convert it into cash. At our meeting with Oxfam we were told that food was needed most of all and transport to deliver it. If we could raise £100,000, we could provide a lorry, 70 tons of rice, 42 tons of seeds and 1,000 fishing nets. Edward's idea of the Great *Blue Peter* Bring and Buy Sale mushroomed into more than 12,000 Bring and Buy Sales nationwide by the middle of December. The bringers as well as the buyers were given *Blue Peter* Cambodia stickers and within two weeks of the Appeal's launch, over twelve million had been distributed. To our total amazement, the £100,000 target was reached in five days.

John Craven films Tina and Christopher Wenner in the *Blue Peter* office, for Newsround

Dear Blue Peter,

Cobbs County Infant School is helping Cambodia to recover from starving. On Blue Peter last week I saw a picture of a little boys bones ribs and I felt really sorry for them. We in England are very very lucky that we have a lot of food and health and living without being starving.

Love Joanne, Warrington

1979

Dear Blue Peter Team,

I'm just an average housewife with a family of four who is very aware of the problems in Cambodia and unfortunately other countries that we don't get to hear about. I'm sure like other wives I'm conscious of the children leaving food on plates etc and nag constantly that there are children starving somewhere.

What has hit me between the eyes this morning – I've just walked in to my daughters bedroom and the enclosed letter is what I've found. I'm sending it to you to show you all at Blue Peter how you are making little ones realise what is happening somewhere else. She must have been thinking about it deeply to write the letter. I know she's very untidy in her writing and she obviously means the following:

'All people in the Cambodia world I hope you do not suffer and (she's missed out we) save your life. Love from Jodie.'

We, by the way, have been to our Oxfam shop and all my girls gave something that belonged to them and bought something.

Best wishes to all that work in the Blue Peter programme,

Yours very sincerely,
Jacky Arnold, Nottingham

1979

Dear Blue Peter,

Last Friday morning our school did a Great Bring and Buy Sale in our hall. We had toys, perfume and lots of jewellery, and books. When we had finished we had £56. As we are in a village we have not an Oxfam shop near us the nearest is Holmes Chapel. All the things we put on the stalls were sold that is why we got a lot of money. The things were all perfect.

Your target in the studio is very high now. So to be fair we put our classess names in a hat and picked out two names. The names were Heather and Jane. So they went to the shop with the money. We got some stickers as well. Before we did all this our class labelled all the things.

Our teacher Mrs. Jones had a secret sum in her mind that was £50 but we went over her sum. Some friends and I went round our block and asked people how many acorns were there in a jar.

We got £3.25 pence We gave it all to our headmaster to give to you.
Yours sincerely,
Alison Watson, age 8 years old, Goostrey County Primary School

1979
Dear Blue Peter,
We are so pleased to hear you are going to do something to help the Cambodian people in your 1979 appeal.

Four months ago, two Cambodian children called Somaly aged 10, and Panita aged 6 came to live near us. They had escaped across the border into Thailand with their mother and Auntie, and were very lucky as a lot of other people they escaped with were sent back to the Khmer Rouge soldiers. Kind people helped them to get to England, where they are now at school with us and learning English fast. We have come to love them a lot, and thought that perhaps all the Blue Peter viewers would like to meet them too, so they will know what nice people the Cambodians are, and that they really deserve help.
With love from Christopher and Catherine, Godalming
At school with Somaly and Panita

1979
Dear Blue Peter,
My sister and I thought you might like to know how many things we collected after hearing your appeal last night.

We collected 40 books, 6 bags, 14 toys and 1 toy bath, 1 light fitting and 3 lamp shades. We found all these things in our bedrooms, a total of 64 objects which is not much compared with all the lives which could have been lost.

Yours sincerely,
Thomasina, age 11 and Charlotte, age 8, Great Yarmouth

1979

To Simon Peter and all the others to the pets Jack Jill and Shep
I have wrote this poem to you so it can go on the bord for to remember the poor people in Cambodia:

Cambodia
Cambodia is a place
A place for all the starvin
Children starve
Adults starve
This place is called Cambodia

This tells that all the people in Cambodia starve but thancks to you they are not meny starving becous you have made enough money to buy everything they need. I go to St Joseps church and I know that all of the people in St. Joseps would like to thank you along with father rion and father Trucy
Yours senserely,
Lynette Fisher, York

1979

Dear Blue Peter,
We had a coffee morning on Saturday 24th November. Our dads helped – one made hot pancakes and the other played ping-pong with the people who came, to see if they could beat him. We had guess the weight of the cake, guess Teddys name and guess the amount of sweets in the Jar. We had two raffles, a baking and a white elephant stall. We hope the £142 we raised will help the people in Cambodia.
Yours sincerely, Kate, age 9 and Susie, age 9, Glasgow

By Matthew Washington

1980
Dear Simon, Peter, Sarah & the Blue Peter Gang,

I think your idea is Great. Last year we went to Wycombe and we got a bargain, a mini snooker table for £2. I'm certain that you will get the money you need. Last year you raised a lot of money and that's proof that you can do it again. I hope you all have a merry Xmas.

Have a happy New Year (I hope the spastics do as well)

Yours sincerely,
John Alan, aged 9, Nr. Great Missenden, Bucks

PS My dog called flash send her fondest woofs to Goldie

1981
Dear Blue Peter Presenters,

I am writing on behalf of a friend of mine she is 9 years old and her name is Julie. She very much wants to hold a Blue Peter Bring & Buy sale and has been pestering her mother to this end. As Julie's mum and myself both work in an Adult Education Institute, we have decided to hold one on her behalf.

You may not think this an unusual request, and you most probably have hundreds of similar ones. The one slight difference is that Julie herself is very special and courageous. She is confined to a wheelchair and is blind she also needs a hearing aid. (She has a disease called Hurler's Syndrome, it is progessive.) She also has to undergo quite painful treatment every few months but all this has not stopped her from wanting to help little babies who are born prematurely and perhaps stop them from having permanent handicaps or help older people's homes be furnished.

So, please send us all the necessary stickers etc. so we can have our "Julie's Blue Peter Bring & Buy Sale" and hopefully raise lots & lots of money for very special people on behalf of a very special little girl.

Yours hopefully,
Mrs. G. Pearce

The Bring and Buy Sale raised a magnificent £2,508.30 for our Appeal. Very sadly, Julie died only a few days after this letter reached us. We wrote to her parents asking if they would accept a gold *Blue Peter* badge in her memory and Mrs. Bennett wrote:

Dear Ms Baxter,
I would like to thank you for the 'Blue Peter' Gold award, given to us in Julie's memory. She would have, indeed, have been very proud, not only of the award, but of the people in Staines who helped to make the sale such a tremendous success. Please let me congratulate 'Blue Peter' upon attaining their target, and the success of the appeal.

I hope, also, that the appeal is successful in increasing society's awareness of the physically handicapped, and recognising the fact that they are people within their own right. May it also encourage the disabled to take their rightful places in society and enable them to do this with ease.
Yours,
Jean Bennett

1981

Dear Everyone at Blue Peter,
I still cannot believe that I am going to receive a new Bec electric chair and its all thanks to Blue Peter. I am writing to thank you all very much indeed.

Having an outdoor chair means I shall now be able to enjoy my independence with my friends, it will be great and of course the Easter holidays are coming up, which reminds me, after Easter I am going with my friend Roger on a Pilgrimage to Lourdes in France. It is the first time I've been on holiday without my mum and dad, and I am looking forward to it so much.

My mum and dad have decided to hold an Afternoon tea party in our local village hall and a Jumble Sale and all the proceeds we will send to Blue Peter. So please can we have a Blue Peter Poster and stickers, if that is at all possible. Thank you so much for all you have done for me and others like me, and perhaps if you, Simon on your way home one day could call in to see us its only a few miles from your part of the world.
Love to all and the new arrivals,
Mark, Chesterfield
PS My mum had to write this letter for me.

1981

Dear Sarah, Simon & Peter,

My son, Robert, saw your programme regarding the Pipeline Appeal from his hospital bed. He had had a major operation, his eighth this year, two weeks prior to the appeal being announced & he started collecting stamps for you. He died on 22nd November aged 19 – his elder brother Peter having died in January this year at 20 from the same rare blood disease.

The enclosed stamps have been collected from letters & cards of sympathy mainly. I thought you'd like to know that Robert was thinking of other people & your appeal, even though he knew he was so ill. Your programme has been followed for many years by Peter & Rob & now by myself & Catherine, aged 18.

Very best wishes,
Mrs. Yates, Keighley

1982

Dear Blue Peter,

I am writing these few lines to let you know that we received the orthokinetics chair on the 21st October for my handicapt brother Jonathan.

I just want to thank you sincerely, words just can't thank you enough for this lovely gift. Jonathan really loves it and mummy says a very big big thank you indeed. It means a lot to us and the day Jonathan got it he sat in it all day.

Love
Sharon, County Tyrone

1982

Dear Sarah, Peter and Simon,

I am sending you some Kissi money wich comes from Liberia. I lived there for a while, and in the villages they use this to buy things with, I hope this little bit of money will help your water supply appeal.

From Richard, aged 10, Norwich

PS Most bush villages in Liberia lack running water & would benefit from water installations

1982

Dear Blue Peter,

When I had collected all the things for your treasure hunt and packed them in a box, I weighed it on our bathroom scales and it weighed roughly 10kg.

So I phoned the Post Office and asked them how much it would cost to send it and they told me £2 90p – I thought, Crikey, that's a bit much, so I wrote to the Post-Master at Harrow Post Office, told him about the great thing you are doing for children, and asked him if there was any way that parcels for your cause could be sent either freepost or at least at a cheaper rate? I waited for a reply and received no answer, so I decided to take it to the Post Office and get it away to you. When I gave it to the lady behind the counter, she said, my word, you have been on a treasure hunt, haven't you.

Anyway, to cut a long story short, she said hold on a minute, and went away – when she came back she said they could send it Freepost!! Wow how about that. I thought that was very good of them, and thanked her, and told her that I would write to you about their kindness.

Yours sincerely,
Mr. J.H. Onyett, South Harrow

1982

Dear Mr. Onyett,

Thank you for your letter and your splendid contribution to our Treasure Hunt Appeal. We hope you saw Blue Peter on Thursday when we announced a nation-wide free delivery scheme for heavy parcels of Treasure. Roadline has again generously offered to deliver these to our Depot and contributions can be taken to any one of its 40 branches.

With best wishes from Simon, Sarah, Peter and all of us on the programme,

Yours sincerely,

Biddy Baxter, Editor

1983

Dear Biddy Baxter,

I was overcome with emotion after listening to the result of your Treasure

TREASURE

500,000

400,000

300,000

200,000

150,000

100,000

50,000

5,000

GLAS

BR

The 1982 Treasure Hunt Appeal for children suffering from kidney failure was an amazing success. Jessie Baxter, age 4, together with Sharon Bassenthwaite, Claire Corps and Rachel Price who'd all made miraculous recoveries, came to the studio with nurses from Great Ormond Street

Hunt last night. Four times your original target of 500,000 parcels has grown to 2 million, it shows what high regard everyone holds your projects in.

I think you & your team are absolutely wonderful. The projects are so imaginative & have helped enormous numbers of people over the years & all over the world. The great thing is that really you are only asking for rubbish, old forks & spoons, used stamps & so on, so that poorer people can help too. In total admiration for you & your team.

Yours very sincerely,
Lisbeth Hildred, Rossendale

In 1983 the Weatherbeater Appeal was launched to raise £250,000 for six of the world's poorest countries suffering from floods and drought. Bring and Buy Sales all over the country ended up raising £1,610,000, providing aid for 21 countries.

1983
Dear Sarah, Simon and Peter,
In this small collection are some of the "precious belongings" of our daughter Sharon and our son Simon. They were killed in a motor accident eight years ago. Sharon was fourteen and Simon eighteen. Our daughter Sarah (who we thank God was saved from the crash) and our little daughter Emma now six, all agree that Blue Peter should have Simon and Sharons 'little collection'. Our best wishes for you and your helpers
Yours sincerely,
Mrs. Raffique, Kenilworth

1983
Dear Simon, Janet and Peter
We are very pleased to hear about your appeal. We have been preparing for a sale for weeks. I have made invitations. Because there are so many people coming we are having it in the morning and afternoon. I have made gift tags and lavendar bags to sell. I am going to make cakes and sweets.
Yours sincerely,
Michael, age 9, Weston-super-Mare

Dear Blue Peter

I have just taken my toys to the Oxfam shop in Wigton and the lady in charge said I was the first person from Wigton to take anything into the shop.
From Stuart, aged 8½, Cumbria

Dear Blue Peter,

I would like to hold a bring and buy sale. As we are going to Australia for a holiday in 3 weeks I was wondering if we could hold it there?

I used to live in Peru and I know very well how poor they were. Except for Cambodia, I am sure that this is your most worthwhile appeal yet.
Michael, Aberdeen

Dear Janet Simon and Peter

Thank you for the autographs from Covent Gardens. I felt excited when I saw you. You looked just the same as when you are on TV. I am sending a pound for your appeal. Seeing you made the best bit in my day in London.
Lots of love
Sarah, age 8 xxx, Leicestershire

Dear Blue Peter,

We heard of your appeal Weather Beater from many of our children, who, enjoy to watch your programme. As we are a school with over forty differ-ent nationalities we decided that this was an appeal that the children could relate to, so we are sending half of our Christmas charities collections to you. I enclose a cheque for £460 and I know it will be well spent.
Yours sincerely,
Mrs. M.P. Jonker-Carroll, The British School in the Netherlands

Dear Mr. Baxter,
I am Charo Lano from Peru, living in Northern Ireland and studying in Dunluce School. Thanks a lot for the badge you sent to me with the thank

you letter for the work that the students did for the Weather Beater campaign. Thank you for what you did for my country. I was very impressed by the way the young people of the UK responded to your appeal. Through the Weather Beater Appeal, teenagers became more aware of the problems of famine, floods, revolutions and wars in faraway lands.

It was very nice to know that even far from home, other people care and are aware of the problems of my country. Thank you for everything.
Yours truly,
Charo Lanao

1984
Dear Blue Peter
My name is Cecilia and I am 6. My daddy and I are english but my mummy is bolivian and as my grandparents still live there we visit Bolivia regularly.

Thank you very much for helping the poor people there, Bolivia is a beautiful country but it is poor and life is very hard.
Love, Cecilia, Kent

1984
Dear Janet, Michael, Simon
During September and October I spent 4 weeks in the Blue Peter Acute Renal care unit at Gt. Ormond St. Hospital London. I had Haemolytic Uraemic Syndrome. There were 4 children in the ward with this disease which is quite rare. We were all in our local hospitals for a week until we were admitted to GOS with kidney failure. The local doctors didn't know the symptoms of this illness. I had a tube in my tummy for peritoneal dialysis but it kept blocking up so I had a shunt put in my left ankle which is a tube inserted into an artery and vein. With this I could be connected up to machines which cleaned my blood. I am going back on the 28th November, to have my shunt removed as my kidneys are working properly.

My parents and I would like to thank you and all the people that helped raise the money for the Blue Peter Unit, which has saved my life and many other childrens.
Thank you, Anita, Canvey Island, Essex

"We picked petals from our gardens. We sold a small handful of petals for 2p, a bigger bunch for 4p and a big bunch for 6p. We've collected 60p."

1984

Dear Blue Peter,

We were watching your programme on Monday and saw Simon in Ethiopia giving out biscuits.

We were pleased to see them because one of the people who invented those biscuits is a friend of ours. She is Miss Pat Disket who lives in Oxford and works for Oxfam.

Yours sincerely
Peter and David Henley, Devize Wiltshire

1984

Dear Blue Peter Presenters,

I am writing to explain to you our schools means of money raising for Ethiopia.

The whole of St. Michael's School, including myself, took part in a fifteen minute sponsored polo suck. We all enjoyed it and, because it was unusual we have already raised over £465. We would like to donate this money to the Blue Peter Life Saver Appeal.

Yours sincerely,
Sarah, Class 8, St. Michael's School, Rossington

1984

Dear Janet, Peter and Simon,

We picked petals from our gardens. We put them in a box which Alison had made. We sold a small handful of petals for 2p and a bigger bunch for 4p and a big bunch for 6p We've collected 60p.

Love from,
Lucy Green and Alison Warner, Edinburgh

1985

Hello!

All the best in the Appeal. This is just a quick note to say why I'm donating £10.00. I sent a 3ft x 4ft Christmas card to my best friend up in Crawley, Sussex on the back I said 'For everyone who signs this card 5p will be donated to the Ethiopian Famine Appeal.

12 hrs later the card has reached Hurstpierpoint, Sussex, with 200 postmen's signatures & hit the papers!

S. Price

1985

Dear Blue Peter,

These keys and braclet were once my late husband who passed away two yrs ago. Age 38. I know if my he were alive he would want you to have these keys to help other people who are in need. The dcs help my husband to have a new life with heart operations 10 yrs ago. He was born a blue baby and they said he would not have a long life. But he was such a jolly person never complained of his illness. I do hope they will be of some use you do such wonderful appeals to help others who are not so lucky as others.

Yours faithfully,
Mrs. S. MacDonald,

my son was very excited to send you something for the appeal and wanted to do you a drawing also of a lifeboat -man!

By William Buffy, aged 4

"The enclosed has been in my sons wallet since he lost his life in a sailing accident at the age of 19. Please put it towards your lifeboat appeal."

1985

Dear Blue Peter,

I enclose a cheque for £100 toward your 'Lend an Ear' appeal. I wish you every success with your fund raising particularly as my young daughter suffers from periods of severe but fortunately temporary deafness, & I have noticed how people's attitudes to her change at this time, & she becomes labelled as 'dreamy' or 'uncooperative' when she simply cannot hear.

Best wishes,
Mrs. Griffiths, Gwynedd

1985

Dear all,

The enclosed has been in my sons wallet since he lost his life in a sailing accident at the age of 19 in 1977. Please put it towards your lifeboat appeal.

Thanks

1985

Dear Blue Peter Presenters,

I am most interested in your appeal this year for Deaf Children, and although 64 an avid fan of Blue Peter. My parents were both deaf and classed as deaf mutes. At a very young age my mother was sent to a Deaf School. I can remember her telling me how unhappy she was to leave her loving family. My Father too attended the school, in those days the only trades they were taught were to be shoe repairers (boys) to go into service (girls).

My reason for writing is to say that both parents had voices which weren't developed or trained. Even I as a child of 3 went to Nursery School to learn to speak as I heard no conversation at home. In spite of all this my parents were wonderful and I had a very happy childhood. Thank you for

your great programme. My parcel will be sent to the depot.
God Bless from
Mrs. Ralph, Sittingbourne, Kent

1985

Dear Blue Peter Team,
I am pleased your 1985/6 appeal is for the deaf. I was amused to find out you are collecting keys as I remember the last time you did this my mother unwittingly sent in the garage keys. My father was slightly annoyed (to put it politely). We still have a padlock on the garage door as a constant reminder and have never let her live it down. She still insists it was for a good cause though. This year we've hidden all our important keys so it can't happen again. I was pleased you told your viewers to check the keys are not being used but this goes to show it is not just children who do silly things!
Sincerely,
Lynne, Kings Lynn

1986

Dear Miss Baxter,
I have been asked by an old lady of 94 called Miss Eakins to send you the enclosed items in the hope that you may be able to include them in any Fund Raising. She has always been very interested in its good work, and has contributed at times. She is nearly blind now and very deaf and arthritic but still takes a lively interest in everything and has an amazing memory.

The little silk apron was sent to her from France in 1914 by a serving soldier in the South Irish Horse, and trained in the City of Limerick where she was born. The necklace was given to her by a schoolteacher except the pendant. The various bits of crochet etc., are pretty ancient too.
Yours sincerely,
Mrs. Field, Belfast

Dear Blue Peter,
On Sat 17th January Boys and Girls of Charlotenburg, Berlin held a bring and

buy sale in aid of your sight savers appeal. A lot of hard work went into this by all children and staff concerned. Please would you accept this cheque on behalf of 1st Berlin Brownies, 2nd Berlin Brownies, 1st Berlin Cub Scouts, 1st Berlin Guides, 1st Berlin Rangers, Charlotenburg 1st School.

Could you please mention all the boys, girls, leaders, teachers and parents who put so much into this worthwhile cause.

Yours in Scouting,
Dave Blackburn

1987

Janet Karon and Mark,
I have reacently reaturned from Mozambique where I lived for two years. I thought that it was appalling that even in the capitol, Maputo there was still not enough food or clothes not even a good supply of water. Peeple in other provinces are starving. I think that you should raise money for Mozambique. I think that you should explain to people that the main cause of starvation is the war which is being waged by South Africa against Mozambique. Mozambican people are good at helping them selfs but need our help as well.

From Poppy Edwards, Bristol

Dear Poppy,
Your mother will have mentioned my telephone call. I tried to phone you the day before we launched our Mozambique T-Shirt Appeal, but had no reply. I do hope you were able to watch last Thursday! We were very pleased to have your suggestion that Blue Peter viewers should do something to help the people of Mozambique. When we consulted our friends at Oxfam, they suggested that the most valuable contribution would be in the form of t-shirts. So far this Appeal has been a tremendous success and you can see film of the T-Shirt Depot, on Thursday's edition of the programme.

With best wishes from Janet, Mark, Caron and all of us on the programme.
Yours sincerely,
Biddy Baxter, Editor

1987

Dear Blue Peter,

Enclosed are some photos of one of the Landrovers bought from your Sight Savers appeal. They were taken by my father, who is the surgeon at the Lodwar hospital in the Turkana District of North West Kenya. I presume the four men are its crew. I hope the photos are of interest to you.

Yours faithfully,
Mungo, Kilmarnock

1988

Dear Mark, Caron and Yvette,

We're writing to tell you that your Rags Appeal is not only helping disabled riders!

At the end of November our grandfather, who we called Tom, died very suddenly and we were all very upset. Now we're helping to sort out his belongings and so far we've been able to send two big boxes of wool and cotton for the Appeal. Doing this has made us feel a lot happier.

Love from Sally, 7ys and Kate, 10 yrs

Blue Peter

Yvette, Mark and Caron launch the 1987 Rags Appeal

1988

Dear Blue Peter,

I am very interested in fundraising for comic relief, the wishing well appeal blind people and desibaled riders. So far I have raised 18p because I only started on 2nd april please could you try and help me get more money.
From Ben, age 8, Pennington

2003

Dear Blue Peter,

We baked jam tarts at our Methodist Church Youth Group and sold them raising £4.10p for the water works appeal. We also raised £5.20p at home from our rude noise pot.
Yours sincerely,
Emily and Harry, Wantage

2003

Dear Blue Peter,

Almost 3 years ago my Dad brought my family here, to Denmark. But living in Denmark doesn't stop me from watching Blue Peter! I watch it on BBC Prime. This year we have to research a project based on humanitarian organizations that help children. My group chose Water Aid and we held a very successful Bring & Buy Sale in which we raised over £600! We hope we have made a difference!
Heather, Copenhagen

2003

Dear Konnie, Matt, Liz and Si,

We are writing to tell you that we have raised an amazing total of £300! We raised this by selling homemade cakes and printed bookmarks at our school. We also visited some other Bring and Buy sales in our area.

Our photo was taken at one of the sales and got on the front cover of the Deeside Piper and Herald. We have enclosed: the money receipt, a photo copy of our newspaper picture and a sample of the 3 different bookmarks

PLEASE read this out on the show and show the picture and book-marks, because our village of Torphins has NEVER been either shown OR said on TV, radio or any other broadcasting type thing. And GOOD LUCK with the rest of the appeal!!!
Yours sincerely,
Naomi, Hannah and Phys

Dear Blue Peter   Liberty Gibson

This money is for you I know its not much but use it well. Please

2005

Dear Sir/Madam

I am writing as the mother of 3 Blue Peter viewers to enquire about your policy regarding disposal of the second-hand clothes from the recent appeal that cannot be sold through Red Cross shops. My children went straight to their drawers and sorted out clothes that they wanted to give, but I have a real worry about the possibility of the clothes ending up being exported to countries in Africa and undermining local industries there.

I would like to know what has happened to the clothes that were not sold, would they have been sold on to merchants who then export them? It would be ironic if Blue peter, whilst trying to support a worthwhile cause in Angola, with one hand, were helping to destroy poor economies with the other. Things are very complicated in this increasingly globalized world.

I look forward to hearing from you.

Clare Churley, North Yorkshire

Dear Clare,
Thank you for your query about what happens to clothes that aren't sold. We of course asked the same question of the Red Cross on our first meeting. They, alongside many other charities, are determined to support the clothing in-

dustry in poorer countries. The unsold clothes from our appeal are sold to the rag trade in the UK. We have been assured by the Red Cross that the ragged clothes never leave the country. This is obviously a topic that concerns you greatly and I can assure you it does us too.

Thank you for supporting the Welcome Home Appeal. I hope you caught Friday's show when Konnie returned to Angola to see how such a simple idea can make a huge difference. With best wishes,

Kez Margrie, Series producer, Blue Peter

Email 2008

About 25 years ago you had an appeal raising money for children with Kidney Disease. The appeal went really well and to celebrate you invited 3 children on to Blue Peter who had recovered from kidney failure.

At the British Transplant Games last year I was speaking to a "Donor Dad", a man whose son had been killed in a road accident and whose organs had been used for transplantation. I asked him if he had found the decision difficult to make and he said "No!". As a young boy his son had watched Blue peter and seen these children speaking about how wonderful life was now that they had had their transplants, and had said to his father that if anything ever happened he wanted to donate his organs!

At this story a shiver went down my spine – I was one of those children, having had a kidney transplant in 1980 (I am now in the top 200 survivors in this country having had my kidney for 27 years!)! the gentleman hugged and thanked me, I asked "Why?". Nothing could save his son, but because his son had watched Blue Peter and that we had shown what a difference transplants can make, some good came out of his death!

I felt you should know this story. Over the years I have told my own story many times to many people and you wonder if it makes a difference. Here is proof that it does! It may not have been immediate but a seed was sown. How many more lives that programme saved I don't know, but at least you know for certain some were. Thank you!

Claire Corps, Dr of Transplant Science, St. James's Hospital, Leeds

[You can see Claire's photograph with Simon, Peter and Sarah on p249!]

Hitting the Headlines

EVER SINCE THE early 1960s, *Blue Peter* has been considered newsworthy. The bad news has always rated more highly than the good but, while it is quite right the programme should be closely scrutinised, when reporting is based on fiction rather than fact, it's important to set the record straight.

On the whole *Blue Peter's* relationship with the press has been harmonious. And often the provincial press has given valuable publicity to the Appeals. But in 1964 it was a recipe that stole the limelight. In November, Dorothy Smith, *Blue Peter's* historian and mother of children aged nine, eleven and thirteen, sent us the recipe for ginger beer that she'd made for countless children's parties and church fetes. It was extremely simple and very cheap – two shillings and sixpence – 12½p in today's money, for eight pints. Not surprisingly, it was a huge success and there were over 9,000 requests for the recipe.

A few days later it made headlines in the *Daily Mail*:

9,000 CHILDREN SEEK TV'S "BEER" RECIPE

More than 9,000 children have asked for a TV recipe for ginger beer which a temperance worker has branded as "a highly dangerous alcoholic concoction". The recipe was given on the BBC's Blue Peter programme for children last week. Announcer Christopher Trace told viewers that anyone who could not get the details down could write in for them. Yesterday the first post brought 9,000 requests to the Television Centre at Shepherd's Bush.

But last night the Rev Robert Tayler, Secretary of the Temperance Union of Great Britain, said: "We are trying to stop the recipe being sent out. I am sending details to the Chairman of my organisation, Sir Cyril Black, MP. We hope he can raise the matter with the Postmaster-General."

Cyril Black asked Robert Tayler to write to the BBC's Director-General, Sir Hugh Greene, which he did, ending, "We understand that this recipe is to be distributed in printed form… and we make an urgent request to you to prevent this ill-considered action. The children and their parents would be quite mistaken in thinking that the resultant beverage produced by this recipe would be similar to that purchased legally and harmlessly in the shops."

Meanwhile, we added a paragraph to the recipe leaflet, emphasising that, as stated, the ginger beer must be diluted and the Director-General replied to Robert Tayler:

Dear Mr. Tayler,
Thank you for your letter about the recipe for old fashioned ginger beer, which was given on our Blue Peter programme. The recipe given was for the traditional and time honoured method of making home-made ginger beer which has been practised in many homes for generations, apparently without intoxicating or other ill effect.
Yours sincerely,
Hugh Greene

There were no complaints from children or their parents. Dorothy's recipe, the correspondence and the numerous internal memos are now in the BBC's Archives Centre at Caversham.

It was almost a year later that the birth of Petra's puppies was featured in the national press and, when she died in 1977, the news was not only in every single national and provincial paper, but the radio and television news bulletins, too.

Two years after that, in 1979, there was massive press coverage when the programme was the victim of malicious accusations that the Appeal for the three million Cambodians in danger of starving to death after Pol Pot's genocide was harming UK charities. The papers had been unstinting in their praise for the Bring and Buy Sales, with stories about the wonderful response from British children, but on December 1st the *Daily Express*, "the paper that cares", ran the banner headline on the front page **"Britain's Forgotten Orphans"**.

A disaffected worker at Dr. Barnardo's gift department was quoted as saying that Barnardo's children would have no presents for Christmas that year because of the success of the *Blue Peter* Appeal. The "charity begins at home" moan is trotted out by some paper every time the Appeal is for people overseas, but because of the scale of the Cambodian Appeal the backlash was raised to new heights. The *Sunday People* went one further: **"Not a Penny More"** was its headline. "The Sunday People today launches its appeal to people of goodwill: 'Please stop responding to the Blue Peter television appeal for the suffering children of Cambodia.'"

Both Dr. Barnardo's and Help the Aged, which was also mentioned, were appalled by the press reaction. Nicholas Lowe, the Appeals Director of Barnardo's, wrote to me: "It is a very great pity that some elements of the media have sought to play off our cause against yours on behalf of the sad situation in Cambodia. This is the last thing we would want to happen. This is not only my personal feeling but one generally held by all our staff."

Hugh Falconer, Director of Help the Aged, wrote: "I can only apologise to you and your colleagues and share with you my distress, dismay and anger that Help the Aged should be quoted in this way."

But the damage had been done. A viewer from Essex wrote:

Dear Sirs,
I was very distressed to read in today's Daily Telegraph the enclosed cutting regarding the Blue Peter appeal and its disastrous affects on our own

CAMBODIA'S GAIN IS BARNARDO ORPHANS' LOSS

By GUY RAIS

So many people have contributed to the BBC's "Blue Peter" appeal for aid to Cambodia that they have overlooked helping Dr Barnardo's 7,000 children this Christmas.

children at Dr. Barnardo's… I and my children have donated to your very worthwhile Cambodian appeal, but when I saw how it was affecting our own children here in the UK I think we are getting our priorities slightly wrong. Please could you do something to right this sad and distressing situation."

An even stronger protest came from Warwickshire:

I was deeply shocked and grieved to read the article in the Daily Telegraph. I can understand and harmonise with the Cambodian appeal, however I feel that after £1 million has already been donated surely the children of our own country could now have a share of happiness this Christmas.

Many charities have suffered a severe blow to their normal supplies this year due to your shortsightedness. I hope this letter will make you realise that you have perhaps been selfish in robbing children of your own country to keep pace with the rest of the world!

1979

Dear Blue Peter,

I am very glad to hear that the Great Blue Peter Bring & Buy Sale has made well over £1½m. But now would you please think about the poor children in Dr. Bonardoes they have NO gifts this christmas. My family and I are giving them half of our presants this year. Who nows some day they may be has happy and lucky as us, and have a very merry Xmas.

Signed Claire, aged 11 yrs, Shrewsbury

1979

Dear Tina Heath, Simon Groom and Christopher Wenner,

I feel I must write and point out that you should now <u>LET IT REST</u> with your Cambodia Appeal. Because of it, a number of the home charities are suffering. Dr Barnardo's – similar children's charities – and the BBC Nation-wide "Operation Christmas", to name but a few. The latter is at present "A DAMP SQUIB".

Moreover, the news last night made it very apparent that the report-ers who have their ears to the ground in Kampuchea, are finding that the so-called "refugees" carrying away the sacks of rice etc. are really KHMER ROUGE PEOPLE!! – so despite what Simon was "allowed" to see when he visited (after all one peasant looks much like another over there) – the stuff is going to the wrong folk.

So, DO try and let CHARITY BEGIN AT HOME and now – with your vast audience – bring home the plight of the needy in THIS COUNTRY!

Yours sincerely,

Mrs. Morgan, Cambridge

PS A common trait of the British is to credit others with the same integrity and purity of thought or purpose as we try to exhibit ourselves, BUT… If you doubt this – just ask the colonials, reporters, and others in the know.

The inspiration for our Great *Blue Peter* Bring and Buy Sale for the Disabled was sixty-year-old Joey Deacon. A remarkable man suffering from cerebral palsy, unable to use his hands, arms or legs and with no powers of speech, Joey had spent 50 years of his life in hospital. He and three other disabled patients, Ernie, Tom and Michael, became friends and Ernie discovered he could understand the meaning of Joey's grunts. It took them one and a half years to help Joey write a book about his life and he achieved international fame when *Tongue Tied* was published and a moving documentary, *Joey*, was made. From the money raised by the book and the film, three specially adapted bungalows were built in the hospital grounds, enabling Joey and his friends to have proper homes of their own. Our Appeal target was to build more bungalows and provide 50 electric cars and two neonatal intensive care units.

Joey's story and his appearances on the programme made a tremendous impact and the Appeal greatly exceeded its target.

Joey Deacon (bottom right) who inspired the Great Blue Peter Bring and Buy Sale for the Disabled with Ernie, Tom and Michael

Dear Simon, Sarah and Peter

I was watching Blue Peter on Thursday 27th of November. I saw how Joey and his frends were getting along in their beautiful bungalow. I would love to help raise some money for disabled people. I know you have to raise £500,000. I belong to a youth group which will have to help you. My mother thinks this is a marvellous idea so please, please send me a Blue Peter Bring and Buy Sale kit.

Yours sincerely,
Louise, aged 12, Wandsworth

Dear Blue Peter,

I hope you are well, I am. I see you on TV on Thurday 27 November 1980 it was all about Jo and all that so please please please help our school to have a bring and buy sale

Love
Ben, Winchester

Dear Blue Peter

I watch you every Monday and Thursday and my dad is a doctor and when I saw Joey at first I felt I immediately should help so I though I should save up my pocket money for 5 weeks my pocket money is 50 pence now so I send this even though Joey is a spastic because a lot of boys in my school think that spastics are dumb I have desinged a flag for Joey (at bottom) so please could you send me a Blue peter set.

Yours sincerely
Daniel, Merseyside

But on June 9th 1983, the magazine *New Society* wrote the following under the heading "Real Joey":

A few years ago the children's television programme, *Blue Peter*, ran a series about a handicapped man called Joey Deacon. Joey was unable to communicate in normal language, but a friend of his claimed to be able to interpret the groaning noises Joey made, and contrived to write his biography. In the usual *Blue Peter* style, an appeal was launched, and much worthwhile charitable work was done as a result.

Joey eventually died, and the programme paid him a moving tribute, with repeat performances of his sad efforts at achieving communication with his fellow human beings. The purpose of all this hard work by *Blue Peter* was to promote a caring attitude to the handicapped in the hearts and minds of the nation's children. But they could not possibly have foreseen the result.

The word "Joey" has spontaneously entered the language of children all over the country. The word is sometimes used as a noun, sometimes as an adjective, thus: "You are a Joey", or "That was a real Joey thing to do", or even "That was the Joeyest thing I have ever seen."

There are obviously echoes of the old usage of "Joey" here (from Joseph Grimaldi, the clown). But it is clear that the children have the Blue Peter Joey in their minds.

Sometimes the word is not uttered at all, and the meaning is conveyed by sound and gesture. The elbows are kept close to the body and forearms waved about in a manic sort of way. At the same time the tongue is used to push forward the part of the face between the chin and the lower lip and a medium-pitched groaning noise is made – "mmmmmm".

Probably Joey himself wouldn't have minded. Children can be verbally cruel when they wouldn't always be physically cruel. It doesn't mean they would necessarily be harsh on the handicapped. But it does mean that, as usual, it is hard to tell just what use the recipients of a media message will make of it.

On June 23rd my reply was published:

Sir,
Contrary to your report in Observations, it was all too easy to anticipate some children might mock the sight and sound of a quadriplegic spastic. We thought long and hard before we featured Joey Deacon on Blue Peter, but because his achievements were so remarkable we took the risk.

The response was overwhelmingly positive. Children asked if others like Joey could be helped and it was entirely due to those requests we mounted our International

Year of Disabled People appeal.

To reject the challenge of helping the handicapped because some children, like some adults, are capable of behaving cruelly, would be negative in the extreme. Parents of a child dying of a brain tumour wrote to say Joey's courage and determination had made such an impact on their son; he identified completely with him. This was far from an isolated reaction.

In purely practical terms, the appeal provided five bungalows for the disabled, 130 electric chairs, neonatal intensive care equipment and incubators for 23 hospitals and equipment for 274 schools and centres for the handicapped. Not a bad use of a media message!
Biddy Baxter, Editor, Blue Peter

The mother I quoted had sent us one of the most poignant letters *Blue Peter* had ever received. Here is part of it:

1981

Dear Blue Peter friends,

Last June, our much-loved little son Richard, after only a short period of illness, had a brain tumour diagnosed. He underwent major brain surgery at Great Ormond Street Hospital and this was followed by a course of radiotherapy treatment at UCH. At this stage he made a very good recovery and returned to his prep school in September. He was a happy and clever little boy and settled back well. Sadly at Christmas he became ill again and what was at first thought to be a virus, turned out to be the agonising fact that the tumour had not, after all, been controlled. Slowly he lost the use of his right leg and arm, and then his left leg and upper left arm. Then he was unable to swallow properly and eventually he virtually lost his power of speech. He never complained, always co-operated and kept his delightful sense of humour till 3rd February 1981 when his Daddy and I drove him to GOS for a previously arranged scan – he never regained consciousness.

Forgive me for writing at length, I do not want this to sound slushy, neither am I seeking publicity but I do want to carry out a wish of Richard's. He and my daughter Lucy 8½ regularly watched Blue Peter. Tina's baby stole Lucy's heart, but Joey and the story surrounding his courage and determination and that of his friends made a tremendous impact on Richard. Of course he started in the last weeks to identify himself with Joey. He even asked me if I could get him an electrically mechanised chair like the boy who played the part of Joey in the film had.

He had planned to write a note (before he lost the use of both hands) and to send his pocket money towards the appeal. After his death on 3rd February I counted the money and he had £4.69 in his safe, so it is with pleasure tinged with great sadness that I enclose a cheque for £5 – knowing this was Richard's definite wish. I should like to write to Joey if you are able to give me his address, for in those last few weeks at home he was my son's inspiration, included nightly in his prayers.
Richard's Mum, Essex

When Joey died in December 1981 there were more letters.

Dear Simon, Sarah and Peter.

Sally Andrew, Christopher Poole (my brother) and myself (Stephanie Poole) are all very sorrow to hear about Joey Deacons death as he was very kind and nice.

Love From

Stephanie Poole,

Sally Andrew and Christopher Poole.

P.S. Give our love to Goldie and Prince

1981

Dear Simon, Sarah, Peter,

When I heard that Joey Decan had died, I cried very much because I care a lot about disabled people. I think Joey Decan had lived a very good life. When I grow up, I am going to help the disabled. I would like to send my deepest sympathy to you all my name is Julia and I am 13 years of age.

London SW14

PS I like your programmes

In 1983 we had a phone call from the Television Centre canteen cashier: "Your garden's a dreadful mess," she said. "I looked out of the window and couldn't believe my eyes!" Neither could we. The canteen overlooks the _Blue Peter_ garden and is always packed with customers – the vandals had obviously come during the night at the weekend.

The garden looked like a battlefield – every plant and shrub had been uprooted, ornaments and sundial smashed, the garden seat shoved into the pond and the whole plot as well as the pond had been covered with black, stinking, gooey sludge – fuel oil.

The pictures looked grim when we showed the extent of the damage on the next programme and there was press and broadcast news coverage too – all resulting in thousands of letters and phone calls offering help. They came from Scotland, Wales, Northern Ireland and every corner of England, making us realise just how much pleasure the garden – designed and built by Percy Thrower with the help of the presenters – had given to the very youngest viewers as well as the OAPs.

1983

Dear Janet, Peter and Simon,

We are so upset at the vandalism in your lovely Blue Peter garden, especially the cruelty to the shoal of fish in the pool, that we want to write to express something of our feelings.

Over the years the programme has given us much pleasure and I had hoped your care for animals and plants would be an example to those who watched. I expect most people do share our joy and interest, and it is heartbreaking to think that there are others who only want to destroy what is good and beautiful. Please accept this small gift towards reparation.

Sincerely,

Mrs. Shill, Cheltenham

Dear Simon Peter and Janet

I was very upset to hear about the vandals who messed up the blue peter garden and put oil in the fish pond I have sent some seeds to help put some colour back into it

Love from Sara age 7, Leeds

1983

Dear Blue Peter,

I was very sorry to hear about your garden being vandalised. I thought I would make some suggestons as to how you could try and prevent the vandles doing it again. It must cost a lot of money to repair the damage so you could start a fund to provide a guard dog to keep in the grounds. Or a security patrol or some barbed wire fences. But I think the dog is the best idea. I enclose £1 to help buy something for the garden or to open the fund.

Yours sincerely,

David, 11, Croydon

one of the dogs I was thinking of

vandle

policeman

"Would you like my goldfish as he is so lonely swimming about on his own."

Dear Blue Peter.

We have just seen what has happened to your garden. Would you like my goldfish as he is so lonely swimming about on his own.
Love from
Emma Howe Age 11.

Lesley Judd and John Noakes begin the vandalised garden clear-up

In 1985, an essay written for a book, *TV and Schooling,* by media studies lecturer Robert Ferguson had wide coverage in the national press. He accused *Blue Peter* of being racist, sexist, royalist and pro-capitalist, and advocated renaming it "Red Peter", suggesting it should have fat, ugly presenters – an idea that provoked a robust response!

1985
Dear Blue Peter,
What a load of ROT some people do talk.
Please, please do <u>not</u> change <u>anything</u> about Blue Peter.
It has always been GREAT and still is.
Please can I have a photo of Janet Ellis who is really lovely,
Yours sincerely,
Paul Morrel

Dear Presenters of Blue Peter,
I hope you will not take to heart the remarks of the pontificating windbag Mr. Robert Ferguson, as quoted in the Telegraph of 1st March.
Yours sincerely,
R.H. Amos, Oxford

Anne Woodward of Kidderminster wrote to the *Daily Mail*:

I didn't know whether to laugh or cry when I read your story about 'Red Peter?' Of all the children's programmes, Blue Peter stands out like a beacon of hope. It encourages the highest principles in a world of declining moral standards and conveys everything that is good educationally.

God help us if the likes of media studies lecturer Bob Ferguson ever achieved power in this country and used children to further such twisted and embittered doctrine.
AW

Dear Biddy & all
How dare this Furguson person say these things about Blue Peter, one

of the best programmes on Children's TV in Great Britain – probably the world & you've got the awards to prove it. I think its sour grapes because his son hasn't won a competition or gained a B. Peter badge.

Neville, Film Traffic

1985

Dear Miss Baxter,

Having read in the Daily Telegraph this week that some clever Dick of a Professor of Media Studies (whatever that may be) feels that your most excellent programme Blue Peter is, amongst other things, anti-feminist, anti-this and anti-that, and that he wishes to put in its place Red Peter!! – may I plead with you to keep BLUE Peter just as it is? It is one of the few really good children's programmes broadcast on any channel. My husband & I, both OAPs find so much to be admired, in both the young presenters, Janet, Simon & Michael, & in the content of the programme, and how anyone can take exception to any of it is quite beyond us.

Yours faithfully,

Mrs. Perkins, Chippenham, Wilts

1985

Dear Blue Peter Team,

I hope you won't take the rantings of Robert Ferguson too seriously. Blue Peter was an oasis of relaxed, entertaining, trustworthy television for our children (now 15-22 years) for many years. We are profoundly grateful that you didn't join the strident Ferguson school of thought and weigh children down with heavy adult problems when they have enough of their own.

As for sexist and racist, I suppose you would need one and a half women and one third of a black person to keep everyone happy! I think the balance is right. If you had two women you would lose a lot of boys and anyway there are more boys than girls in the country.

So keep up the good work and God bless you

Yours sincerely,

Anthony Bush, Chairman, Bristol Family Life Association

Dear Sir/Madam,

After reading an article in today's Daily Mail concerning Blue Peter, I felt moved to put pen to paper (as I am sure many more were) in defence of this excellent children's programme.

As an ex-Blue Peter viewer I find it very reassuring that I can let my 4 year old watch it unsupervised, as the programme can be relied upon to inform in an easy and informal manner, and, more importantly, to "set an example". Television today is a very influential medium, and I feel strongly that it has a duty to today's children.

Finally, to criticize the yearly Blue Peter Appeals is, I believe, grossly unfair. My daughter was upset by the pictures of Ethiopia & religiously cut stamps off envelopes every day feeling she'd done something to help. If this helps sharpen her awareness of others less fortunate than herself, then I for one will not complain. Please keep up the good work!

Yours faithfully,

Mrs. Watson, Clwyd

In 1987, several weeks after Janet Ellis had told viewers she was expecting a baby, a former colleague from her days as a journalist on her local paper made enquiries about her pregnancy. Janet misguidedly trusted him, believing their conversation was to be off-the-record, only to be rewarded with the screaming headline in the *Daily Mail*: **"Blue Peter's Unmarried Mother To Be"**, a huge photograph and a piece of flip, gossipy reporting that mocked the programme and made Janet out to be selfish and uncaring.

The *News of the World* was quick to pitch in the following day with an "exclusive" feature **"Blue Peter Jan Faces Baby Outcry – Marry at once or quit"**. The latter, explained the *News of the World*, was the reaction of the then Tory MP for East Leicester, Peter Bruinveals, who was quoted as saying that Janet should realise the bad example she was setting and that children should have a fair start in life, which meant being born in wedlock.

The story was repeated and embellished the following week in the *Express*, *Daily Mail* and *Daily Mirror* as well as in countless provincial papers including, predictably, the *Leicester Mercury*, which carried another Peter Bruinvaels interview in which the MP pronounced Janet Ellis should get married or resign. By now the story, such as it was, had become even more distorted. It was revived in the *Daily Mail*'s letters column the following week in a letter from the Isle of Wight headed **"Not in Front of the Children"**. This accused Janet of a lack of concern and deliberately publicised the fact she was unmarried. The letter concluded: **"Any parents and teachers are concerned about the decline in moral and ethical standards, and it is unacceptable that Ms Ellis should parade her lack of standards before millions of children. Blue Peter has always presented good programming that you could trust would educate and entertain children. That trust has been betrayed."**

A great many readers obviously believed every word of these reports. There was an outburst of protests criticising Janet, but some letter writers rose to her defence.

Dear Janet,

I have watched Blue Peter for over 25 years since I was about six and now my three children are avid and regular viewers.

I think it is very unfair the press have made such a fuss over you not being married to the baby's father. I cannot see how this can affect your job as a presenter, my children have certainly not enquired as to your marital status! It is a shame that scandal-seeking reporters should intrude on your private life.

I wish you lots of luck for the future and advance congratulations for the birth of your baby.

Best wishes,

Georgina Lawrie, Portsmouth

Another mum from a Leicester council estate wrote a furious letter to me:

I am appalled at Peter Bruinvals wanting Janet to quit... it's up to Janet not Bruinvals, how dare he interfere. We love Janet on the programme and can't wait to know what her baby will be.

But others were severely critical. One man who wrote to me sent copies to the BBC's Director-General, the Prime Minister and the Home Office:

Are the young girls who watch your programme to be led to believe that having bastard babies in this day and age is quite in order? Mind you, the present Director-General is not setting a good example... Apparently you are "delighted" with this disgusting news and it may be you who should consider resigning instead of attempting to draw a veil over the affairs.

None of the critical letters sought to question what they had read in the press or to distinguish the newspaper reports from the "Not in Front of the Children" letter. I thought that maybe we were receiving letters from a very gullible and naïve section of the public. But two months later, probably the worst letter of all was written by someone who scarcely came from the gullible category. It was from a bishop's wife and Liverpool's Diocesan President of the Mothers' Union, who had been a fellow student at Durham University. The writer said she "hadn't seen the programme", as though a complete "Janet's pregnant" documentary had been transmitted. She said she had chaired a conference and shared the concern of the members who had evidently discussed Janet and *Blue Peter*. The members felt betrayed and in the bishop's wife's opinion, **"it seems a pity to highlight an intelligent, privileged woman who deliberately decides to have a baby and bring it up without benefit of a father. So many of the problems we are left to deal with in the Mothers' Union are the result of experiences of one-parent families, through marriage break-up or unmarried motherhood".**

I replied saying I was sorry the bishop's wife and the Mothers' Union members had chosen to believe salacious reports in the press. The truth was that Janet had made one mention of her pregnancy, some months previously. No further details of her private life were given, which were of no concern to anyone other than Janet's immediate family. I corrected all the inaccuracies in the letter, ending: "It saddens me that certain members of the Mothers' Union should take such an unchristian attitude about the news of a new life."

The bishop's wife did have the grace to apologise. She said she had no idea the gossip had originated from press reports, or that the declaration that Janet was not going to marry the baby's father had not been made on TV.

Inevitably, the whole affair blew up again in June, after the last *Blue Peter* of the series, and yet again in September, after Janet's son had been born. On June 29th the *Daily Mail* ran their **"Blue Peter Bosses Axe Unwed Mother Janet"** story, although they knew quite well that was rubbish. Once more lies were being printed and in yet another effort to put the record straight, Janet wrote to the Letters' Editor:

I wasn't axed says Blue Peter's Janet

I WAS surprised to read in the Mail that I'd been 'axed' from Blue Peter. If that's the case, I'm still waiting for my letter of dismissal!

I am leaving the show, after four very happy years, to pursue my career — and have a baby. After a smashing 'last' programme (there are two Janet Ellis specials coming up in the next two weeks), we all bid fond farewells at a hugely enjoyable party.

I'm looking forward to showing Blue Peter viewers my new baby and editor Biddy Baxter has invited us both on to the show in September.

JANET ELLIS,
BBC, Television Centre,
Wood Lane,
London W.

Presenter Janet Ellis

There are doubtless some *Blue Peter* viewers who still believe Janet was dismissed thanks to the lies perpetrated by the press. And from time to time the tired old canard re-emerges – even in the 21st century!

The headlines have continued to be hit by *Blue Peter* and the spotlight has mainly focused firmly on the presenters. Eight years after he had left the programme, in 1994, allegations about John Leslie's private life were reported in the national press. A court case followed and John was found innocent, but sadly the bad publicity put an end to his television career. He is now a successful property developer.

In 1998 Richard Bacon was exposed by a Sunday newspaper for taking drugs only seventeen months after he had joined the team. Richard resigned but gradually returned to broadcasting and has made a great success of his own show on Radio 5 Live.

The editor of *Blue Peter*, Richard Marson, was the victim of a misguided attempt to keep a live transmission going during the breakdown of the phonelines, when the result of a competition was being broadcast. A junior member of the production team panicked and asked a studio visitor to use an internal telephone to give their answer, which won the prize. When this regrettable deception came to light a year later, Richard was moved from *Blue Peter* but remained in the Children's Programmes Department.

Six months later, it was reported that there had been another incident over the naming of the new *Blue Peter* kitten. This time Richard was not to blame. He had been so concerned about the accuracy of the online votes, he made an editorial decision that the kitten (with its four white paws) should be named "Socks" rather than "Cookie". This was widely reported in the press and, after an investigation lasting nine months, Richard was sacked from the BBC. He had worked on the programme for ten years and was an inspired editor. His dismissal in 2008 was a great blow to the programme.

Competitions

COMPETITIONS HAVE BEEN an important ingredient of the programme from its earliest days. But it wasn't until 1963 that, to be absolutely fair to every viewer, they were divided into three age groups: sevens and under; eights, nines and tens; and tens and over. First, second and third prizes are awarded in each section and on occasions when there has to be an overall prize-winner, the judges choose between the three first prize-winning entries.

There is always a closing date, in order to give competitors who live far away from Television Centre just as much chance as those who live nearby. The presenters always help the production team with the judging, together with invited guests. For instance, Phil Redmond, creator of *Grange Hill*, helped to judge the entries for a new storyline for the series. Entries are shortlisted by the *Blue Peter* office and, on the judging day, the names and addresses of the entrants are kept secret until the final decisions have been made. Before the names of the top prize-winners are announced, the parent or guardian of each entrant is telephoned to check that the entry is the competitor's unaided work.

As well as the top prizes, there are competition badges for all the runners-up and often a special souvenir of the competition. In 1988 the 2,000 York Minster Bosses competition runners-up each received a certificate signed by the Dean of the Minster, together with a genuine piece of the wood that was saved from the flames that destroyed the south transept roof. Each piece was branded with the York Minster shield and the *Blue Peter* ship.

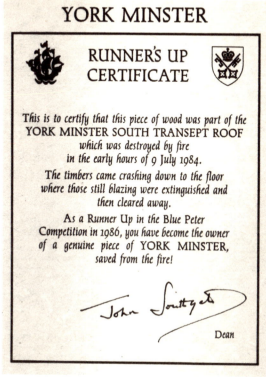

It is so important to be fair, but occasionally people have cheated. In *Blue Peter*'s first-ever cartoon competition, "Picture of Health", celebrating the 40th birthday of the National Health Service, after the results were announced, there were hundreds of letters and phone calls saying that one of the top prize-winning cartoons had been copied from a magazine. Some viewers sent the magazine as proof. It was horrible, not only to have to break the news to the cheat's parents but also to arrange for the prize, a bicycle, to be returned. We had to mention this on the programme because so many viewers had complained, but we did not divulge the person's name or where they lived. We felt it would be wrong to pillory a child on network television. Unfortunately, the local paper did not have the same scruples and featured the story, in spite of pleas from us not to do so.

The competitions are extremely popular. Those involving drawing and painting attract the largest numbers of entries. And often the most imagina -tive pictures are from the youngest viewers, who express themselves naturally without adults telling them how to be artistic. Guidance from teachers, although very well intentioned, can inhibit the imagination. Some- times entries from gifted children have been astounding – like the intri- cate and colourful design that won ten-year-old Lucy Butler a top prize in our Natural History Museum Centenary poster competition in 1981

Sarah Greene with Lucy Butler and her prize-winning poster

The top prize-winner in the elevens-and-over section, Amanda Taylor, painted a dinosaur with its back full of lit birthday candles. It wasn't until her design had been chosen that Amanda was revealed to be a child with Downs Syndrome. Although she was fourteen, she had a mental age very many years younger than that and it was suggested (not by her family!) that it would be too risky to include her in a programme transmitted "live" and not recorded. I disagreed. Amanda's parents were happy for her to take part and I knew the presenters would treat her lovingly. As it was, when Amanda arrived in the studio, it was Simon's dog Goldie that broke the ice. Amanda ran towards her with open arms crying "Goldie!" at the top of her voice. After that we all relaxed, and you can see from the expression on her face that Amanda loved her visit to the studio. The prize-winning posters went on show.

Amanda Taylor was the top prize-winner in the elevens-and-over age group

1981

Dear Blue Peter

I had a really exciting day yesterday, all because of your poster competition. We got up very early so that we reached London by 9 in the morning. The sun shone all day. I thought London was brilliant, especially when a pigeon sat on my head. We saw the changing of the guard and had a picnic too, then rode on escalaters and tube trains to reach the Natural History Museum.

We looked hard at all the lovely posters and wondered how you managed to choose mine. Then we saw the huge whale and pressed buttons in the mammals hall before we went home. Now mum and dad say we can have another day out to do different things. I hope lots of other families are having happy days out like ours just because of your programme

Love from Philip, Matlock

1960

Nursery Rhymes Spot the tune
1. Sing a song of sixpence
2. London Bridges Broken Down
3. Old King Cole.
Lillian, aged 11, Perthshire

Dear Lillian,

You will probably have heard that you have won a prize in our Spot the Tune competition in Blue Peter. I am sending it to you now, and I hope you will like it.

Yours sincerely,

John Hunter Blair,

Producer, Blue Peter

A competition in 1966 gave *Blue Peter* viewers the chance to design the first-ever Christmas stamp. It was a double first because it was also the first time stamps had been designed by children. The two winners were both six years old – Tasveer Shemza from Stafford and James Berry from Bromley, Kent. Their designs – the head of one of the Three Kings and a snowman – were copied 183 million times! On December 1st, the day they were issued, Tasveer and James came to the *Blue Peter* studio to be presented with gold badges.

Fifteen years later, another Christmas stamps competition was announced; this time the winning designs were copied 500 million times. But Mrs. Cross of Glasgow was furious and wrote an angry letter to the *Radio Times* which Sarah Greene read out on the programme in January 1981:

I am writing for a number of people to express disgust at the idea of having some rubbish put on our Christmas stamps again, as in 1966 – a 'design' by six year olds. What can a six year old know about a suitable design for the chief occasion in our Christian calendar? They were a disgrace to go round the world. After buying my first dozen I stuck to the Queen's head.

If Blue Peter (and who are they – trained artists or designers?) have any sense, they'll put an age below which no attempts will be considered. If there's a whole year's preparation, let us hope for something better than that hideous face with a crown, an insult to the central figure of Christmas.

In the intervening years the designing has been taken over by some of the country's leading designers. Why not let them continue and save our blushes? What other country would put out a six year old's scribblings?

1981

Dear Blue Peter,

I was upset to hear of the comments of Mrs. Cross in the Radio Times. I would have thought that as she obviously thinks she is a 'good' Christian, she should remember that we celebrate the birth of a child in this time, and that Christmas is more than anything a time for children. Why not let a child design the stamps? I thought the 1966 designs were super, and if my own 3

year old daughter was able to paint a picture for you this year I would be only too pleased. I wish you every success with your competition.
Yours sincerely,
Lisbeth Stedman, Chelmsford

In 1979, the International Year of the Child, *Blue Peter* was asked by the Post Office if viewers could design a picture for the official First Day Cover envelopes. The winner of the first prize in the sevens-and-under section was five-year-old Adrian Cresswell of Stourbridge, with his colourful trainload of children of all nationalities and the puffs of smoke from the engine billowing out the message, "Year of the Child 1979". This cheerful design became the overall winner and Adrian and Lesley Judd went to the printers to see it rolling off the presses.

Dear Lesley,
Thank you for going round the printers with me. I had fun and I like my First Day Cover. We took the big bag of stamps to Kidlington on the way home.
Love from Adrian xxxx
X Simon X Goldie X Chris X Jack X Jill X Biddy

Later in 1979 Adrian's design was used on the First Day Cover to commemorate the centenary of the Conwy Valley railway. A copy was sent to us by the Llechwedd Slate Caverns.

Another winner wrote:

1979
Dear Simon, Chris, Lesley and Biddy Baxter,
I hope you are all well. Thank you for your letter. I got it this morning. I really enjoyed coming to the studio and meeting you – it's one of the best things that's ever happened to me. Lots of my friends had seen me on tely, so when I went to school everyone was pleased with me & wanted to know what it was like. I will always treasure the medal and the stamp album (I collect stamps now). Next time I watch Blue Peter I will remember what a lot of work has to be done before this ½ hour programme goes on to the air.

John Noakes, Christopher Trace and Valerie Singleton with Joey and Patch and entries for the Come to Britain poster competition

Thank you again for being so kind to me and giving me such a lovely day.

Love from Gwinear xxx, Gwent

PS my sisters send their love

PPS I am sorry to hear that Lesley is leaving. We will miss her very much.

PPPS I've just been interviewed for the local newspaper about the competition and we did have a lovely journey back, thank you, despite the snow & ice.

GOODBYE AT LAST – GWINEAR xxxx

1978

Dear Biddy Baxter,

What a delightful surprise my son Daniel had this morning when the letter arrived advising him of his position as runner-up in the Goldie limerick competition and enclosing his third Blue Peter badge. Daniel had in fact not been the least bit interested in the first prize, wishing much more for the postcard of Goldie. His first competition-winner badge was gained when he was four and entered the Expo 75 competition. He was a runner-up there, and was one of the chosen few whose paintings went on exhibition in Japan. The second badge was as runner-up in the Silver Jubilee competition. You can therefore imagine how proud he is to have done the triple. His only wish now is that you held more competitions so he could have a chance of becoming Collector of the Week (of Blue Peter badges) on Swap Shop!

Yours sincerely,

Glenda George, Yorkshire

1982

Dear Biddy Baxter, Sarah, Simon, and Peter,

Thank you very much for the smashing day at the Blue Peter studio, my dad and me really enjoyed ourselves. I am looking forward to my trip in a private jet. While we were at the studios my dad told Derek Freeman [Guide Dogs for the Blind Puppy Walking Manager] about my dog Christy being poorly, on Tuesday she died.

Thanks to Derek Freeman I now have another dog, a springer spaniel and it goes on lots of walks, it's a great dog. Thanks for a day I will never forget.

Yours sincerely,

Geoffrey, Cleveland

292

"Thank you for the Brill 'Blue Peter'... Everything stops in our house when it is on!!!"

1987

Dear Biddy Baxter and all the 'Blue Peter' Team,

I was very surprised and excited to find out I was one of the runners-up in the 'Blue Peter' Railway of the Future Competition and to get the special wallet and 'Blue Peter' competition badge. I will look after them and treasure them always. I was sure I would not win a prize because the other children's pictures and ideas looked so good on the programme.

Thank you very much for the lovely prizes and also for the Brill programme 'Blue Peter'. Everything stops in our house when it is on!!!

Lots of love from Helen, Southampton

Caron, Yvette and Mark with the top prize-winner of the Design an Outfit for Caron competition, eleven-year-old Jasmine Nealon

1987

Dear Ms Baxter,

I'm writing to you whilst the memory of delighted amazement that I saw on my 4 year old Jonathan's face is still fresh. He was one of the top Runners Up in your Railway of the Future competition. Although he worked very hard on his entry, spending over an hour concentrating on his own – a long time for a small child, I did not imagine he had a chance. He, however, expected the train set to be delivered by return of post! I did persuade him that he probably wouldn't win and so the letter came as a wonderful surprise. Thank you for organizing your competitions so that a large number of children can tell they have succeeded.

Yours sincerely,
Valerie J. McCartney, Liverpool

We received 32,373 designs for new bosses to replace those destroyed by the fire at York Minster in 1984. We asked viewers for ideas showing important happenings in the twentieth century and the most popular themes were outer space and the Concorde. It was thrilling for the winners to know that – unless there was another fire – their great-great-great-great-grandchildren would be able to see their designs turned into carved, painted bosses fixed into the roof, for centuries to come. This caught the imagination of viewers all over the country.

Three of the top prize-winning designs for the York Minster bosses

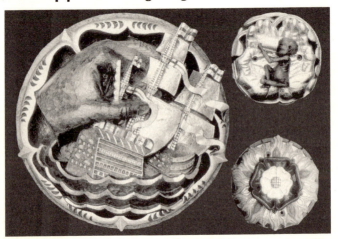

1988

Dear Simon,

My Dad came over here from America to work for 3 years.

We went to York Minister on a visit and I saw two Blue Peter Bosses waiting to go up. I saw the diver and the whale on 1 boss and the badge on the wall.

I like watching Blue Peter on BBC1.

From Brian, 8 yrs, Cheltenham

On Friday November 4th 1988, Her Majesty the Queen attended the Service of Rededication at the Minster. Her Majesty inspected the bosses high up in the superbly restored roof and spoke to each of the six winners who had been invited to York for the ceremony.

1988

Dear Blue Peter,

Last Thursday my 4th year GCSE History group went to London for the day, visiting the Wellcome Institute Museum, as we are studying the history of medicine. You may remember that in 1984 I was one of the 24 lucky winners of the Annual competition, and attended the "Blue Peter Party". I had a fabulous day out.

Anyway, on the return journey, by train, from London, I saw a Mr. Lloyd and his son, returning from this year's party. I told them that I had been a winner four years earlier, and they showed me their souvenirs. It really made my day!

I just wanted to thank you again for choosing me. I shall remember it always as one of the happiest days of my life.

Lots of love,

Helen, Cheshire

In 1998 two Blue Peter Promenade concerts celebrated the programme's 40th birthday and viewers were asked to design the front cover of the Proms programme for the entire season. Here is ten-year-old Sarah Dunn from St. Andrew's at the Albert Hall with her programme:

To Blue Peter

Thank you for giving me tickets for going to your prom. I enjoyed every minute of it! My favourite part was when the mystery musician came and played Chinese fireworks X! Another good bit was when all the players in the orchestra came on late and when Stuart and Richard and Konnie all honked the horns. THANK you for signing my programme and getting lots of other people to sign it to.

Love Sarah

By Sarah Dunn

The ingenuity of viewers who entered the competition to design a really useful robot in 2001 amazed Dr. Jeff Johnson, the Open University's Senior Research Fellow in Design and Innovation. He and his colleagues scrutinised every one of the 32,035 entries. "We had such a variety of robots – gardeners, policemen, litter pickers, a huge range of rescue robots and hundreds of robot mums!" The top prize-winners had working prototypes of their robots built. Their prize was a trip to Japan for the International Robot Games Festival.

Ruth Montgomery of County Antrim, who won third prize in the elevens-and-over group wrote:

> ### Dear Blue Peter team
> I'm just writing to say thank you very much for the lovely art set you sent me, as my third place prize. I'm sure it will come in very handy, and it will be well used, I assure you. I'm really pleased with the Blue Peter Badge and I can't wait to try it out.
> ### Yours sincerely,
> ### Ruth
> PS Your new puppy is really REALLY REALLY cute!! I was going to send you a doggy treat but my mum wouldn't let me in case the bomb disposal unit think it's dangerous.

In October 2002 there were no age groups for the competition to design an outfit for Liz. She was to wear it playing the part of Venus in *Club Blue Peter*'s Christmas extravaganza. The announcement of the competition results led to this complaint:

> 2002
> ### Dear Blue Peter
> My Complaint
> On the 14.10.02 when you announced the winner of the dress competition you picked two people from the same age group and it was appauling. You onley toke 6 min to get through with it and did not announce the 100 runner-ups.

I entered the competition and wasn't expecting to win the competition but it might have taken people about half an hour to finish it.

Yours sincerely,
Emily, age 7½, Kent

2002
Dear Emily,
Thank you for your letter. I'm sorry you were disappointed by the results of our dress design competition. As Blue Peter is a magazine programme, full of different items, we never give more than 6 minutes to the results of any competition – even one as brilliant as this one. We did look at every single entry and we could see how much work had gone into your entries – as Liz said on

Matt Baker, Simon Thomas, Konnie Huq and Liz Barker in a dress designed by a viewer

the show. This wasn't a competition with separate age groups – Liz simply picked the ones she thought would be best to wear in the show. The standard was really high throughout all ages though. Watch out for the finished designs and a feature in next year's Blue Peter annual.

With best wishes from all of us on the programme.
Yours sincerely,
Richard Marson, Series Producer

The enthusiastic responses to the competition to choose a BBC child presenter in 2003 resulted in this anxious exchange of emails:

Email 2003
BBC Child Presenter
My son, Andrew, entered the competition to be a BBC child presenter. He worked very hard to create a video which he sent to you. Since then he has

heard nothing. I understand you may have received a large number of entries but he is desperate to find out if he's been successful. He rushes to check the post every day and some kind of response would be very welcome.
J. Rogers

Email 2003
Thank you for your email. Yes we have had a huge response. Unfortunately we cannot reply to every single entry. However the results will be announced on October 15!
Blue Peter

Email 2003
I was delighted to see that my son Andrew had won one of the 45 prizes in this competition. He was so excited to see an excerpt from his tape appear on television, and to see his name on your web site. (I must admit I was a little jealous, as I never succeeded in winning anything as a child!) However, he has not received any confirmation of this, nor the book and badge that were promised on the programme. Andrew is a very patient child, but is finding it hard to understand why he has to wait so long to hear from you. I would therefore be very grateful if you could let me know when he might expect to receive his prize.
Many thanks & best regards,
John Rogers

Email 2003
Dear John,
Thank you for your email. We are so sorry about the delay. We are still in the process of getting the books signed and hope to send the prizes out in the next couple of weeks.
    With best wishes from everyone on the programme.
Blue Peter

Email 2003
Thank you for your swift reply. I am however very unhappy about this lengthy delay, which displays quite a casual approach towards the thousands of children who participate in Blue Peter competitions, and who at the very

least deserve the courtesy of a rapid response. I would therefore be grateful if you could send me the name and contact details for a senior member of the BBC to whom I may complain.

Regards,
John Rogers

Email 2003
Dear Mr. Rogers
Your email has been passed to me as Editor of Blue Peter. I'm sorry you feel so strongly that we have displayed a casual approach to children who took part in our competition. I can assure you that this couldn't be further from the truth. We have a small but highly dedicated team who have many years experience of turning round competitions like these. In this case I should imagine the chief problem has been the recent postal strike which has caused havoc with all our mail. Very unfortunate but as I'm sure you will appreciate, not a situation over which we had any control. I do hope Andrew will enjoy his prize when it finally reaches him — he did very well indeed!

   With best wishes from all of us on the programme,
Richard Marson, Editor, Blue Peter

Email 2003
Dear Richard,
Thank you very much for your reply. I very much appreciate the fact that you have taken the time to reply to my complaint. And before I go any further, I should say that Andrew did indeed receive his prize yesterday. I may have sounded a bit curmudgeonly in my complaint, and if this is the case then I'm sorry. I'm sure you have a great team dealing with the competitions, and all of their replies have been both polite and prompt.

   Andrew loves Blue Peter. He's quite determined to obtain one of the 'full' Blue Peter badges, in one way or another, and he's hoping that if he sends enough letters to you then one will be read out.

Best regards,
John Rogers

PS

In 1943 my late husband, John Hosier, who was then fourteen, wrote to BBC Radio's *Children's Hour*. He had been thrilled by the dramatisation of John Masefield's *Box of Delights* and wanted to know who had composed the music played throughout the series. Here is the reply he received:

The British Broadcasting Corporation
Broadcasting House, London W1
31st December 1943
Dear Sir,
We are delighted to know that you enjoyed "The Box of Delights" so much. Here is a list of some of the music which was used in it:

A Carol Symphony (sometimes called "Noel Fantasy") by Victor Hely-Hutchinson. The "Boy" music was the introduction to 'Variations on a Nursery Theme' by Dohnanyi. 'L'Apprenti Sorcier' (Dukas) 'Pictures at an Exhibition' (Moussorgsky) Symphony No. 1 (Szostakowicz).

We are interested to hear your view that the Children's Hour is less popular than it was a few years go. I think this is probably partly due to the war. In peacetime listeners could hear Children's Hours on six different wavelengths. Now there is only one, and we are reduced, as you know, from an hour to forty minutes. This inevitably results in less variety. Many good broadcasters are in the Forces and can only come rarely to the microphone. When peace returns we will certainly have more scope.
Yours faithfully,
May E. Jenkin, Assistant Children's Hour Director

No marks at all for calling a child "Sir"; it's certainly not in the style we would use today. But full marks for the content and for taking my husband's comments so seriously. He certainly treasured the reply enough to keep it amongst his papers for 66 years.

Nine years after John's correspondence, this letter was in the *Children's Hour* postbag. May Jenkin (Auntie Elizabeth) was by then the head of the department:

Dear Miss Jenkin,
Is it possible for my brother Corin and myself to have an audition please?

Uncle Mac says that he has already telephoned to you about us, and that you are expecting a letter from us.

Corin is 12½ and I am 15½ yrs. Neither of us have had any really serious training except for some coaching from Daddy, and a very little extra for myself, but perhaps Uncle Mac explained that.

About what we can do: we are both in our school choirs, I have been in all our school plays, if that counts for anything; Mole in "Toad of Toad Hall", Joan in "St Joan" and Herod in a Nativity play by Dorothy L. Sayers.

We can both speak (or think we can speak) various dialects, Corin can do American, Welsh, Northumbrian and West Country; I can speak Italian fairly fluently and with the right accent, besides American, Welsh, Scottish and Irish.

Corin is going to Public School in the autumn, so, just supposing we succeeded at the audition, he would only be able to do anything at weekends or in the vacations; anyhow that's presuming too much.

I do hope this letter has said everything that ought to be said, you wouldn't believe how many times I've written it out!
Yours sincerely,
Vanessa Redgrave

This commitment to children right from the early days of broadcasting was a rich heritage for those of us working for the same audience in television.

Was it worth it? After standing down as Head of Children's Programmes to return to his first love of film directing, Edward Barnes wrote to the team: "As you might have guessed, *Blue Peter* is very special to me. Not only because I worked on it for so long, but because at its best, it represents the pinnacle of achievement of this department. It has probably given as much warmth and happiness and sense of belonging to individual children – as membership of their own family. Because uniquely – that's what it is – a twice weekly family get together."

I felt exactly the same in the summer of 1988 when I too left the programme. The following, unprompted letters all came from the heart as do so many of the letters and emails to *Blue Peter* in the 21st century. They are just a fraction of the postbag received and reinforce my belief that I was the luckiest person in the world to have worked for the world's best audience – children!

"I was washing the kitchen floor, when the postman came with a large envelope from the BBC! For a split second I wondered who had written to me from such high places!"

1988

The Editor – Blue Peter

I've watched you all – from Lesley Judd
to Val/Janet – and Sarah.
I've watched them shine in Sun; through mud
as Caron – there's none fairer!

But Biddy Baxter, I declare
(without a chance to meet her) –
remains my BP Golden Share –
The Editor – Blue Peter!

Best wishes,
Norma

1988

Dear Biddy Baxter,

I was washing the kitchen floor, when the postman came with a large envelope from the BBC! For a split second I wondered who had written to me from such high places! Then I thought Biddy Baxter, and I hastened to open up and find the beautiful photo and lovely letter enclosed. I watched you on TV say how you would answer all letters in time but never dreamt I would hear so quickly. Thank you, thank you, for your kindness, you have made my day, as never in a million years did I expect so much. I just wrote to say how I've enjoyed the programme, because you deserved it after doing so much for so many over the years, and lets face it, these days we don't hear enough of the good deeds done by people, do we, far too much time given to the bad people, in our lovely world.

I feel like Queen Bee, everyone is going to be green with envy ha ha. I do part time hairdressing, four afternoons a week, all the old dears between 70 and 80 walk round to Mrs. Brown, for a hair do, and that super photo of my friend Biddy as I now look on you, will sure be shown to them all. With such a boost to my morale this morning I may even pass my 3rd grade piano exam at 11 am tomorrow! I've passed I and II so far, you see you can teach old dogs new tricks, it will be five years in November, since I started.

With renewed thanks to you Biddy, for your great kindness in writing to me so soon, and for the photo, which I will treasure always, and I also hope, that if you ever come to Suffolk, or wish to come, there is a bed here at 'Adderbury' for you. Just phone and say I'm on my way! Ha again best wishes to you from the Brown family.

Yours sincerely,
Mrs. Brown, Bury St. Edmunds
I repeat you're a lovely lady, no kidding

Dear Biddy Baxter,
May I wish you good luck & excellent health for your future, after such a long time at the head of "Blue Peter", surely a great success story under your guidance. You have given me hours of happiness over many years, & I have had charming answers to several letters I have written to you in the past.

I sent you a photo of my Teddy Bear once, disputing the claim that the one on your programme was probably the oldest, but mine was a rival to that title. I am now semi-housebound, being in my 85th year, but young enough in heart, & with several great-grandchildren to appreciate your pre-sentations for the younger generations.

From the beginning I collected the "Annuals", & the smaller books about Valeries travels. I retain, still, four large scrap books recording so many pro-grammes, & cuttings – & your letters & postcards of your presenters – & pets. Eventually I will pass them on to go with the Annuals – to remind my descendants of a fantastic programme for children, during this century – I hope the high ideals you have maintained will go on as before as a tribute to your dedication. I wish you well, & success in your next venture.

Yours very sincerely,
Mrs. Barber, Bridport

Dear Mrs. Barber,

Thank you for your sweet letter of 25th June. I appreciate all your kind remarks about me and Blue Peter and I'm delighted to know how much pleasure the programme has given you over the years.

How lovely that you have kept so many Blue Peter books and made-up your own scrap books about the programme. I'm sure your grandchildren will look after and treasure them for many years to come.

Please don't worry about the future of the programme. I'm hoping my deputy, Lewis Bronze, will take over from me and if he does, I know the programme will go from strength to strength! Lewis has worked on Blue Peter for 5 years so he knows all the things the viewers like best. I hope you will continue to watch and enjoy the programme.

With renewed thanks for taking the trouble to write and best wishes from all of us on the programme.

Yours sincerely,

Biddy Baxter, Editor Blue Peter

1988

Dear Blue Peter

I am very sorry to hear that Biddey Baxter will be leveing soon. So I rote this letter sending my love to her. I can just imagin how she will feel. So do you think you could say how sorry I am. I think she must work very hard to get things ready. Blue Peter is my very best program. Also I wish it could be on every day.

On Monday 20th June we made some food called Baked bananas. Me Nicolas Julie and Nathan made it. We didn't make it on our own Mrs Smith a helper helpd us. On Tuesday 30th March 1988 it was my birthday I am 7 now. The last time I rote to you I was 5. My school work is very good. At least that's what my teacher said to me. Anyway that's all I can think of for now.

Lots of love
Danielle, Hertfordshire
PS Give my love to Biddy Baxter

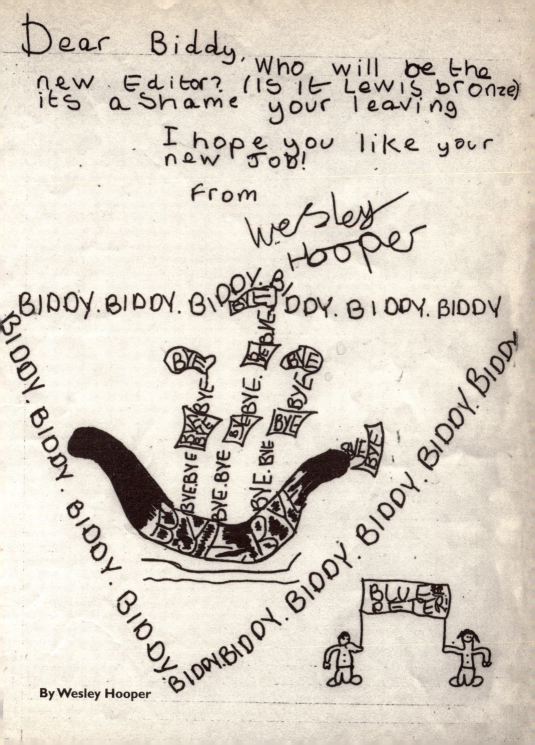

Dear Biddy, Who will be the new Editor? (Is it Lewis bronze) its a shame your leaving

I hope you like your new Job!

From

Wesley Hooper

By Wesley Hooper

Dear Biddy Baxter
     I'm sorry to hear that your Leaving. But I'LL hope you will find A great New job Good Lukk. And Best wishes.
from
Alexander John Bishop!

1988

Dear Miss Baxter,

Other than writing a book about Blue Peter, you didn't say what else you are going to do.

Surely, my guess may be right, "Our BIDDY" is 'gonna get wedded', as the yanks say.

Am I right Biddy?; Because you're still an attractive woman.

Best wishes for the future, I hope it all goes O.K.

Yours affectionately

J.W. Carrington

The Old Age youngster (65), Bedford

BYE
BYE
BIDDY
with love
from Edward
Laverick
and here is one
I made earlier

1988

Dear Mrs. Baxter, Mark, Yvette and Caron,

Thank you very much for bringing me so much joy on Monday and Thursdays, I have been watching Blue Peter for as long as I can remember, and hope to go on watching forever.

To prove that I have been watching BLUE PETER for ages, I remember drawing a dinosaur for one of your competitions over 5 yrs ago I have also got the sledge instructions and I made the sledge from them, but somebody pinched it.

I thought that a monkey would make an original pet to go with Bonny, Willow and the tortoise. It must have been a terrible shock to you when you heard that Percy Thrower had died, even though I am 13 I cried for ages, as he seemed such a thoughtful, loving, considerate kind person. And, I know you all loved him.

Just because Mrs. Baxter is leaving doesn't mean that there will be no more Blue Peter does it, as I love the places you go and the competitions you set. Even if, for some absurd reason, you are told to stop the program

Percy Thrower, who designed the Blue Peter garden, with Janet and Simon measuring the giant sunflower

due to price cuts, tell them that I, Adam, 13 will pay.

　　GOOD LUCK BIDDY. FIREWORKS BLASTING YOU OFF, WISHING YOU LUCK WITH YOUR NEW JOB.

Your loyal fan, Adam, Liskeard

RSVP

1988

Dear Miss Baxter,

Just one more tribute to your excellent work as Editor of Blue Peter over all these years. I was on holiday, hence the delay in writing.

　　Apart from my pleasure in seeing a woman doing a good job and being seen to do it, the quality of the Blue Peter programmes has been excellent all the years I have watched them – since I got a TV in 1962 or so. They give pleasure and are educational to a wide range of viewers without in any way talking down to them. I am 76 years of age, retired principal Lecturer in a College of Education, and I get so much pleasure out of "Blue Peter".

　　In one way, I am sorry for your successor! for you have set such a high standard, but I wish her/him well. Whatever you do now I am sure you will do it well, and I wish you joy and success in it. Thank you very much.

Yours sincerely,

Nancy Anderson, Belfast

Throughout the years there were so many letters that boosted the morale of production teams and presenters alike. Here are some that made us feel very close to our unseen audience:

1972

Dear Biddy and you all, in front and behind the camera, who work so hard and with such a loving care to produce the "Blue Peter" programme.

　　I am writing this letter to thank you for the pleasure you give to so many young children and their mothers, including myself and my two.

　　Especially I would like to thank you for your kindness and thoughtfulness in answering to both of my children's letters, individually. They treasure your letter and going to keep it among their few precious possessions. We are foreigners, or better still, from "overseas", living in your country and loving here as our own. Wishing you all a very happy 1972

With love
Mrs. Petmezas, Southall

Lesley Judd and John Noakes, Valerie Singleton and Peter Purves rehearse a dance routine

1972

Dear Peter and Val and John,

You may think it strange to get this letter, but I wanted you to know how much you delighted my son, Adam, who died just before Christmas. He was absolutely devoted to your programme and his insistence made us send off the parcel of cotton and wool for your appeal, as it had always prompted us with other appeals!

He was a marvellous companion, a great wit, and had indomitable courage. He was born with a very serious heart malformation but <u>never</u> in the nine years of his life did he <u>ever</u> complain of his misfortune! He was very bright and clever, and earned the nick-name "Hawkeye" as one could never hide anything from him!

In April 1970 we took him to America for major heart surgery, and there he nearly died – but with characteristic determination he fought back, holding on to life. The operation seemed to have been perfectly successful and these last two years Adam has gone from strength to strength. Attending Highgate Junior School, first and second in his class, trying new things like swimming, and running upstairs! He has always shown enormous confidence and hope for the future, and although life must have been a series of frustrations and disappointments he never showed it – but always fought on with an arrogance and wit that were impossible and charming!

He died very suddenly on 21st December when playing a normal happy game with his brother and sisters. It was all over in half an hour, but he knew he was dying and said "I suppose I'm going to die! I just want to go to bed to sleep." He was very peaceful in the end, slipping away in a coma.

Television was his greatest joy – for there he could run and climb with John, make Val's useful gifts, or meet interesting people like Pete. We thank you so much for the happiness you gave him.

Yours sincerely,
Mrs. Reddington, London NW3

1975

Dear John, Peter and Leslie,

I felt I just had to write and thank you and all others concerned with Blue

Peter for the years of entertainment your programme has given to me. I have been watching Blue Peter now since 1964, when I was 7 years old. In all this time, I have missed only a handful of programmes and I have never yet been disappointed by any of them. Unfortunately, I soon start working and shall not be able to continue watching regularly, although I shall look in when possible. Many thanks once again from a completely satisfied viewer,
Yours sincerely,
Stephen, Southend-on-Sea

1983
Dear Blue Peter,
Many congratulations on your 25th Birthday. I have enjoyed the show since the early sixties, and at 23 I still watch it today.

It's difficult to put into words the appeal the show has for me. But I think it's something to do with the fact that you never talk down to your viewers. Blue Peter is a programme that children watch rather than a chil-drens programme. Being an only child I was at times desperately lonely, and there were few things that helped to alleviate that but I am pleased to say that your show did help. Your show, and Patrick Troughtons version of 'Dr. Who' had a strange way of making me feel good.

In June 1977 I visited the States, and had the great pleasure of attend-ing two Elvis Presley concerts. It was something that I will never forget as long as I live. But I tell you this the joy I felt at seeing 'Elvis' in the flesh was nothing compared to the feeling I had as a child when your theme music came on.
Joe, Aylesbury

To Blue Peter
Thank you very much for a splended and wonderful day with you in your studio, it was really great fun. Thank you for putting up with me and for sign-ing your autographs for me. My brother also wants to thank you, he says "Thank you everybody on Blue peter for giving my sister a memeral day of her life and thank you for signing your autographs for me as well, bye".

It was my first day ever to even pass by the BBC centre and I was really nervous about it when we arrived you made me feel so welcome that I forgot all about my nerves and I relaxed a little bit. I will tell all my friends at school that I saw Blue Peter in the studio 4 running live for the television programme. Anyway thank you all very much for inviting me to the studios and for making me feel so welcome when I arrived.

All my love
Cheryl Gimey

Presenters and camera crew waiting for the countdown cueing another "live" edition of the programme

Janet Ellis in *Blue Peter's* 1987 Christmas spectacular

1987

Dear Ms Janet,

I have watched Blue Peter since Valerie Singleton's days and after seeing your Christmas Variety I couldn't resist sending you this copy of myself taken 80 years ago. It appears there is nothing new under the Sun and Moon.

Congratulations to you all, on your wonderful programmes, and your bravery on occasions, to make it all so interesting.

Do not bother to reply or return photo (just a little joke).

Yours sincerely,
Dorothy

Dorothy aged 3, 1903

"I wonder if, at 83, I am one of your oldest 'fans' right from the first programme till now without missing one broadcast?"

1987

Dear Ms Baxter,

Along with my two daughters, Katherine and Amy who are aged nine years and thirteen years, I have just watched your Blue Peter review of 1987.

We have few regular viewing spots, but Blue Peter is one programme we rarely miss. I have watched Blue Peter since being a child and my own children have their own enthusiasm for the programme which transcends any parental influences. As I watch I am often amazed at the range, simplicity and constant quality of the programme. It is topical, non-patronizing and yet still innocent.

Can I offer my thanks as a parent and also as a dedicated viewer for your extremely fine programme. A happy new year to you and your team.

Best wishes,
Mr. Hawthorn, Lichfield

1993

Dear Miss Baxter,

I wonder if, at 83, I am one of your oldest "fans" right from the first programme till now without missing one broadcast? But, its me, Blue Peter means Val, John & Peter. Petra Goldie and Jason the Siamese cat evoke precious memories & when the BP garden was destroyed I felt as if my own place had been desecrated.

I helped my children & grandchildren collect paperbacked books, keys, etc for various charities, seen Goldie as one of the famous dogs at Crufts – the variety is endless. I don't suppose I'll be around for your "Golden" Jubilee so thank you for all the pleasure you gave to children of all ages. By the way I've never made any models which turn out like the ones shown.

Yours sincerely,
Mrs. Luker, Epping, Essex

1992

Dear Biddy,

I am writing to thank you and Hilary for looking after me so efficiently on Tuesday last when I attended the Director General's Seminar for Science.

On my return home, my wife spotted one of your letters amongst all of my documents and immediately brought out an old and battered envelope from her collection of memorabilia. I enclose a photocopy of the letter it contained – I think you might find it somewhat amusing! Apparently Valerie Singleton had implied that hamsters were smelly and this had invoked an indignant outburst from the 12 year old Miss Maureen Robins who simply signed herself as "A Looker In". Her parents were totally unaware of her actions until your reply popped through the letter box. I guess you must have had to write many conciliatory letters of this nature during your time with Blue Peter.

As we still have the original letter, you have two courses of action to stop us "going public". Either you send vast quantities of used ten pound notes to the above address, or you promise to contact me next time your business brings you to Oxford and permit me to invite you to dinner at Merton College.

With best wishes to yourself and Hilary,

Yours sincerely,

Lawrence Harwood, Merton College, Oxford

Enclosed letter:

1966

Dear Looker In,

Thank you for your letter.

You are quite right – if they are looked after properly, as you look after yours, hamsters do not smell. Valerie meant to say that they could get smelly if they were neglected.

With best wishes from Chris, Valerie, John and all of us on the programme,

Yours sincerely,

Biddy Baxter, Editor, Blue Peter

"What's been your most memorable moment on *Blue Peter?*" is a question that often crops up and is almost impossible to answer. But it has to be May 10th 1976 when Otto Frank took part in the programme.

It came about by the most amazing chance. Filming a documentary on Amsterdam in his *Blue Peter* Special Assignment series, Edward Barnes had included Anne Frank's story. Months after it had been transmitted, he received a letter from an uncle of Anne's saying he had been visiting Britain and seen the programme, would it be possible for Anne's father Otto to have a special viewing? None of us had realised Otto Frank was still alive. He was the only one of Anne's immediate family to survive the concentration camps and by now was well into his eighties. Edward arranged a viewing and when Otto Frank saw the film, he said it was the best portrayal he'd ever seen of Anne's story.

Edward had assumed that Anne's original diaries were no longer in existence, but Otto Frank told him the exercise books had been put in the vaults of a bank in Basel for safe keeping. "Herr Frank," said Edward tentatively, "would you consider removing one or two of the volumes to show the children of Britain on *Blue Peter*, should you ever return to the UK?" To his delight, Otto Frank agreed and it wasn't long before his tall, erect figure was walking across the floor of Studio Three at Television Centre, holding the precious diaries.

Lesley Judd was naturally apprehensive. How easy would it be to communicate? How could she expect someone in their mid-eighties, being questioned in a different language about the brutal death of his daughter and wife, to react to the hurly-burly of live TV? In the end it was Otto Frank who put Lesley at her ease. He was courteous, dignified, understanding and, most remarkable of all, completely without bitterness or rancour. As he turned the pages of the exercise books covered with Anne's neat handwriting, he translated: "In spite of everything, I still believe that people are really good at heart. If I look up into the heavens, I think that it will all come right, that this cruelty will end and peace and tranquility will return again."

"The spirit of Anne is alive," he said. "There is the Anne Frank Foundation. Each week I receive many letters from children of Anne's age and younger, from countries all over the world. Anne's story has given them courage and a conviction that there must be no more fighting, no more war. Anne did not die in vain."

It was miraculous that Lesley did not break down. We were all in tears in the control gallery. Even the camera crew and the technicians felt a sudden need for their handkerchiefs. There was not one of us who did not feel the better for meeting Otto Frank. He was quite the most remarkable human being ever to have taken part in *Blue Peter*. Neither Lesley nor any of us on the team could believe our eyes the following week when, amid the hundreds of appreciative letters from children, there were a dozen or so from adults castigating us for inviting Otto Frank to *Blue Peter* and containing obscene reprints of the *Myth of the Six Million* broadsheet claiming that the extermination of Jews in Hitler's gas chambers and concentration camps was an invention, that no genocide had been perpetrated in the WWII and that Anne's diary was a hoax.

The MP Sir John Stanley raised the issue with the BBC's Director-General, Charles Curran, who firmly rejected the complaints and we were cheered by the many supportive letters we received in 1976 and again when it was repeated in 1987.

1976

Dear Peter, John & Lesley,

My husband & I were watching Blue Peter last week with our children when Mr. Otto Frank visited the studio. We felt what a joy & a privilege it was to meet him in this way. It was hard to believe all that he has gone through in his life. We felt that we could see in him the very characteristics which we all admire so much in Anne.

We also wanted to express our appreciation of the warm & sensitive way in which Lesley interviewed Mr. Frank. Thank you.

Yours sincerely,

Mrs. Brown, Bridgewater, Somerset

1987

Dear Biddy Baxter,

I was watching the edition of Blue Peter which showed a clip from the interview with Otto Frank talking about his daughter Anne Frank's diary. I myself have read the book which is brilliant. It is also sad because I am Jewish and lots of people from my family were killed in the Holocaust by the Nazis since they lived in Poland and Lithuania. But an amazing fact is that my second cousin who now lives in Israel was in Amsterdam during the war, but even more amazing was that he was in Anne Frank's class during the war and actually proposed to her!

When the Nazis came him and his whole family survived by going into hiding, hidden by his school teacher!

Yours sincerely,

Miriam (age 11), Kingston upon Thames, Surrey

Have children changed during the last 50 years? In many ways they are exactly the same. The response to the Appeals this century has been equally enthusiastic as it was to those first toy collections in the early 1960s. Children are still passionate about "fairness", still tend to see issues in black and white with no shades of grey. They still regard the presenters as their friends and the pets truly have remained substitutes for many children unable to have pets of their own. Paul Bulger of Reading summed it all up in his letter of 1987:

Dear Blue Peter,

I enjoy your programme a lot. I am thirteen and just about to go up in the third year of secondary school. Your programme helps me a lot because every time you do a film on old houses and famouse people I always jot notes down for when we do a prodject at school. It has helpt me all ready because we done a prodject on the seonde world war and I wrote about Anne Frank. Most of the information I got was from Blue Peter and I got an A minus for that piece of work. I also like the part where you do some cooking every time you do some cooking I am always ready with a pen to write down the ingredents. I'm keen on railways and I like the Blue peter railway. But I haven't seen it for a long time so please could you bring out the railway again. I also like the new presenters espescialy Mark as he is always cheerful and makes jokes. I like caron because the way she dresses and the way she makes jokes with mark. Ive got to admit I fancy caron a lot.

   Keep up the good work
Paul Bulger

Biddy Baxter with Yvette Fielding, Mark Curry and Caron Keating

Appendix I
Blue Peter Presenters, 1958–2008

Christopher Trace
16 October 1958 – 24 July 1967
Died 5 September 1992

Leila Williams
16 October 1958 – 8 January 1962

Anita West
7 May 1962 – 3 September 1962

Valerie Singleton
3 September 1962 – 3 July 1972
(last regular appearance)

John Noakes
30 December 1965 – 26 June 1978

Peter Purves
16 November 1967 – 23 March 1978

Lesley Judd
15 May 1972 – 12 April 1979

Simon Groom
15 May 1978 – 23 June 1986

Christopher Wenner
14 September 1978 – 23 June 1980

Tina Heath
5 April 1979 – 23 June 1980

Sarah Greene
19 May 1980 – 27 June 1983

Peter Duncan
11 September 1980 – 18 June 1984
& 9 September 1985 – 27 November 1986

Janet Ellis
28 April 1983 – 29 June 1987

Michael Sundin
13 September 1984 – 24 June 1985
Died July 1989

Mark Curry
23 June 1986 – 26 June 1989

Caron Keating
13 November 1986 – 22 January 1990
Died 13 April 2004

Yvette Fielding
29 June 1987 – 29 June 1992

John Leslie
20 April 1989 – 20 January 1994

Diane-Louise Jordan
25 January 1990 – 26 February 1996

Anthea Turner
14 September 1992 – 27 June 1994

Tim Vincent
16 December 1993 – 24 January 1997

Stuart Miles
27 June 1994 – 21 June 1999

Katy Hill
23 June 1995 – 19 June 2000

Romana D'Annunzio
1 March 1996 – 20 February 1998

Richard Bacon
21 February 1997 – 16 October 1998

Konnie Huq
1 December 1997 – 23 January 2008

Simon Thomas
8 January 1999 – 25 April 2005

Matt Baker
25 June 1999 – 26 June 2006

Liz Barker
23 June 2000 – 10 April 2006

Zoe Salmon
23 December 2004 – 25 June 2008

Gethin Jones
26 April 2005 – 25 June 2008

Andy Akinwolere
28 June 2006 –

Valerie Singleton and
Christopher Trace in 1966

Appendix II
Blue Peter Pets, 1962–2008

Petra, mongrel: 1962–1977

Fred(a), south European tortoise: 1963-1979

Jason, seal point Siamese: 1964–1976

Patch, son of Petra: 1965–1971

Joey, Brazilian blue-fronted parrot: 1966–1968

Barney, Brazilian blue-fronted parrot: 1968–1969

Shep, Border collie: 1971–1987

Jack and Jill, twin silver spotted tabbies: 1976–1986 (Jack), 1976–1983 (Jill)

Goldie, golden retriever: 1978–1992

Maggie and Jim, south European tortoises: 1979–1982

George, spur thigh tortoise:1982–2004

Willow, Balinese variant: 1986–2005

Bonnie, daughter of Goldie: 1986–2001

Kari and Oki, rescue centre cats: Kari 1991–2006, Oki 1991–

Mabel, Border collie cross: 1996–

Lucy, golden retriever: 1999–

Meg, Border collie: 2001– (left with Matt)

Shelley, Mediterranean spur thigh tortoise: 2004 –

Smudge, rescue centre cat: 2004–2005

Socks, rag doll cat: 2006–

Cookie, rag doll cat: 2008–

Peter Purves cared for Petra before her retirement

Appeals

TARGET	RESULT

1962 and 1963
Toys for children who would have no other Christmas presents

Enough toys to distribute to children all over Britain

1964 – Guide Dogs for the Blind Appeal
3 tons of silver paper and foil to provide 1 guide dog

7 ½ tons of silver paper providing 2 ½ guide dogs and funds to maintain a brood bitch

1965 – Tractor for Africa Appeal
15,000 parcels of wool to provide a tractor for Uganda's Bugosa Farm School

45,000 parcels, providing 1 tractor, plus 1 disc plough, rotavator, rigger and fuel and maintenance

1966 – Blue Peter Lifeboats Appeal
60,000 paperback books to provide1 inshore lifeboat

240,000 paperback books providing 4 inshore lifeboats

1967 – Houses for the Homeless
120,000,000 stamps to provide 2 flats for homeless families

750,000,000 stamps providing 8 flats

1968 – Nigerian/Biafran Civil War Children's Appeal
144,000 parcels of wool and cotton to provide a hospital truck taking medical aid to the starving children and babies

2,000,000 parcels providing 3 hospital trucks, 6 emergency doctor's cars, 2 jet injectors, 6 rehabilitation trucks

1969 – Old People's Bus Appeal
60,000 parcels of old model cars and brass to provide a bus for housebound elderly people

500,000 parcels providing 4 buses, 40 high-backed armchairs, 15 baths with lever taps, 15 mini fridges, 18 ejector seats, 6 TV sets, 2 power-glide wheelchairs

1970 – Holiday Caravans Appeal
200,000 parcels of spoons and forks to provide 3 8-berth holiday caravans to give 1,000 children an annual holiday

2,250,000 parcels providing 3 caravans plus a specially adapted log cabin and a gift of 2 steel homes

TARGET	RESULT

1971 – The Starehe Boys' Centre Appeal

3,000,000 parcels of woollen socks and cotton pillowcases to provide 1 dormitory for the Starehe Boys Centre, Nairobi

6,000,000 parcels providing 2 fully equipped dormitories with places for 60 boys

1972 – Old People's Centre Appeal

£7,000 worth of "treasure" to provide 1 old people's day centre

Over 225 tons of treasure providing 2 old people's day centres plus 8 hot-dinner vans and 100 holidays

1973 – The Blue Peter Stampede for Ethiopian drought and famine

2,000,000 envelopes of used stamps to provide 300 oxen, 150 ploughs, 12 tons of seed to enable refugees to return to their village of Dinser

Over 6,000,000 envelopes providing 400 oxen, 200 ploughs, 12 tons of seed and an irrigation scheme in the Danakil desert

1974 – The 3 B's Appeal

2,000,000 envelopes containing 2 ounces of buttons, buckles and badges to provide 1 guide dog and 1 block of kennels

Line 3 extension to hospital blocks at Forfar and Bolton, an isolation and maternity block at Leamington, automatic drinking system at Exeter and an incubator at Tolgate

1975 – The Clothes Horse Race Appeal

200 tons of old wool and cotton to provide1 fully trained pony for the RDA plus equipment for 300 centres

Over 800 tons providing 21 ponies, an indoor riding school, 16 tack rooms with special ramps for wheelchairs, 10 field shelters, plus 20 wheelchair ramps

1976 – Lifeline-Lebanon Appeal

2,000,000 envelopes of old stamps and postcards to provide a 3-month extension of the stay of the British medical team, 10 tons of dried milk plus 99,000 doses of vaccine for the sick children – victims of the Civil War

Extension of the stay of the medical team, 10 tons of milk, 99,000 doses of vaccine plus 2 tons of special food re-equipping of the Ajazzi Hospital plus a training centre and nursery

1977 – The Key Note Appeal

2,000,000 parcels and envelopes of old keys and toy cars to provide 4 mobile classrooms for deaf children

2,500,000 million parcels and envelopes providing 4 key-note vans plus video equipment for schools in Northern Ireland

TARGET	RESULT

1978 – Medi-Bike Appeal

Used postage stamps and pre-decimal and foreign coins to provide 400 Medi-bikes for health workers in Tanzania

Over 1,000 Medi-bikes plus additional medical care for children and babies

1979 – The Great Blue Peter Bring and Buy Sale for Cambodia

To provide1 eight-ton lorry, 70 tons of rice, 42 tons of seed, 10,000 hoes, 1,000 fishing nets

£4 million providing 57 eight-ton lorries, 27,000 gallons of diesel, 2,300 tons of rice, 5,500 tons of rice seed, 310,000 hoes, 3,000 tons of fertiliser, 1,000 fishing nets, 10 tons of fishing net twine, 1,000 doses of vaccine, 82 tons of yarn to weave cloth, 200 irrigation pumps, 30 tons of plastic for utensils, 18 days hire of DC10, plus a ferry across the Mekong

1980 – The Great Blue Peter Bring and Buy Sale for the Disabled

To provide 4 specially adapted bungalows for disabled people in England, Ireland, Scotland and Wales, 50 electric cars for adults and children, 2 neonatal incubators for newborn babies

6 bungalows at Caterham, Belfast, Lanark, Cardiff, Eastry and Sunderland plus 1 Blue Peter flat in the YMCA's Helen Graham House in London, opened by HM the Queen, 15 Ortho-kinetic chairs, 2 neonatal incubators based in Newcastle and Birmingham, neonatal equipment for 23 hospitals across Britain, 50 electric cars, equipment for 274 schools across Britain

1981 – Operation Pipeline Appeal

2,000,000 envelopes of used stamps and pre-decimal and foreign coins to provide pure piped water for 2 villages in Java

5,025,000 envelopes and parcels providing 150 pure water systems and health care services for 150 villages in Java

1982 – The Treasure Hunt Appeal

500,000 parcels of "treasure" to equip a ward for emergency kidney cases at Great Ormond Street Hospital for Sick Children and to help 11 other hospitals nationwide

The Great Ormond Street Ward plus running costs for 3 years. Also: equipment for 30 other hospitals, 5-year grants to Renal Social workers plus running costs for a holiday centre for kidney patients

1983 – The Weatherbeater Appeal

Bring and Buy Sales to raise £250,000 for 6 of the world's poorest countries suffering from floods and drought

£1,610,000 providing aid for 21 of the world's poorest countries helping approximately 1,000,000 men, women and children

TARGET	RESULT
1984 – The Double Lifesaver Appeal 800,000 envelopes of old buttons and post-cards to replace Blue Peter's 4 lifeboats plus 800,000 envelopes of stamps for 4 irrigation schemes for Ethiopia, 9 water tanks, 30 tons of wheat, a 10-ton truck, 220 tons of molasses	All 4 Blue Peter lifeboats replaced plus 2 additional boats. In addition to the Ethiopia target: 15 water tanks, 6 water pumps, 330 latrines, plus a well digging scheme
1985 – The Lend an Ear Appeal 1,000,000 envelopes and parcels of old keys, foreign and pre-decimal coins and scrap metal to provide 10 radio hearing aids, Blue Peter Hearing Aid Lending Library N.B. the Blue Peter Lending Library for Deaf Children was the first of its kind in Europe!	3,500,000 envelopes providing 10 radio hearing aids and the Lending Library plus 70 radio hearing aids for the library and a full range of environmental and communication aids
1986 – The Sightsaver Appeal Bring and Buy Sales to provide 2 mobile eye units for Malawi manned by ophthalmic as-sistants plus training for the assistants	£1,600,000 providing mobile eye units for Mozambique, Nigeria and Tanzania as well as Malawi plus 2 medical motor-bikes. 2,000,000 people in West Africa had their sight saved during the next 7 years
February 1987 – Emergency Appeal T-shirts for Mozambique	T-shirts for Mozambique's victims of war – one million T-shirts in less than one month
1987 – The Rags Appeal 1,000 tons of old wool and cotton to replace the pony Rags (from the 1975 appeal) plus equipment for 635 RDA groups	2,300 tons of rags provided the pony Jet plus 10 more ponies and equip-ment for every RDA group
1988 – The Great Blue Peter Bring and Buy Sale for Cambodia Bring and Buy Sales to raise £150,000 to repair the 200 irrigation pumps and the ferry across the Mekong provided by the 1979 appeal	Repair of 200 pumps, the ferry re-pairs plus the building and equipping of a pump maintenance workshop and school to train electricians and welders
1989 – The Baby Life Appeal 10 million aluminium drink cans to provide equipment for 16 Special Baby Care Units	40,000,000 cans providing special equipment for 65 hospitals across the UK

Mark, Caron and Yvette with the Totaliser for the 1987 Rags Appeal to replace Rags the pony (from the 1975 Appeal for the RDA)

TARGET	RESULT

1990 – The Bring and Buy Sale for Romania

£625,000 to provide 8 orphanages with laundries and kitchens, teams of volunteers to advise orphanage staff plus 50 family-style homes

£6,582,534.35 providing laundries and kitchens for 25 orphanages, 12 houses plus a nursery nurse training course and a foster parents scheme

1991 – The Golden Age Appeal for the Elderly

15,000,000 aluminium cans to provide alarm buttons, a telephone alarm response centre, a care and repair service plus the expansion of day centres in Arbroath and Belfast and the first incontinence advice and laundry service in west London

19,000,000 aluminium cans
All projects funded

1992 – The I-Care Appeal

Bring and Buy Sales to provide £100,000 for two Land Rovers and moped units for people suffering from river blindness in Mali

£1,289,172
All projects funded plus additional aid for West Africa

1993 – Pieces of Eight Appeal

Collecting "booty" (broken jewellery, old postcards, etc) to replace the 6 Blue Peter lifeboats

All 6 lifeboats replaced and lifeboat number 7 was provided for Fishguard

1994 – The Well Water Appeal

Bring and Buy Sales to raise £350,000 for 185 tube wells and to repair 393 old hand pumps to provide clean water and sanitation for 166,000 people in India, Pakistan and Bangladesh

£1,568,806 providing clean water and 1,649 new wells and 8,350 lavatories in 825 villages

1995 – The Paperchain Appeal

5,000 tons of junk mail to provide 100 lightweight or electric wheelchairs for disabled children in Britain

8,500 tons providing 385 wheelchairs

1996 – The Great Bring and Buy Sale for Leprosy

Bring and Buy Sales to raise £500,000 for 15 mobile treatment units, motorcycles and bicycles for nurses and doctors, a clinic in Brazil

£2,635,405 providing help for thousands more sufferers in Brazil and India

TARGET	RESULT

1997 – The Cystic Fibrosis Appeal

Bring and Buy Sales to raise £500,000 for 50 portable nebulisers, 50 mobile oxygen kits and 50 mini trampolines for physiotherapy, 2 specialist mobile nurses plus a day care centre

£2,045,000 providing day care centres in Manchester, Cambridge, Bristol and Dundee plus 6 nurses and extra specialised equipment

1998 – The New Future Appeal

500 tons of aluminium, foil and cans to provide 3 schools for the children of Mozambique

Enough foil and cans to build the 3 schools plus an extension to a school in Gurue

1999 – The New Life Appeal

Bring and Buy Sales raising £500,000 to replace the hospital equipment provided by the Baby Life Appeal in 1989

£2,303,683.95 to equip 115 neonatal units plus three specialist ambulances

2000 – The Stamp Aid Appeal

100,000 envelopes of used stamps to provide health care for 12 communities in the High Andes in Peru

187,000,000 stamps providing health care for 21 communities plus a Blue Peter Training and Support Fund, bicycles and a medical van

2001 – The Wheel Help Appeal

Bring and Buy Sales to raise £500,000 for minibuses and mobility scooters for isolated elderly people

£1,013,104.32 for minibuses and scooters in England, Scotland and Wales plus similar projects in Northern Ireland

2002 – The Waterworks Appeal

Bring and Buy Sales to raise £500,000 to provide clean water and sanitation for communities in Tanzania and Uganda

£1,431,000 providing help for 78,000 people

2003 – The Get Together Appeal

Bring and Buy Sales to raise £500,000 to train volunteers running school clubs for children with learning problems

£750,000 raised – all projects funded plus additional aid provided

2004 – The Welcome Home Appeal

25,000 bags of used clothes to raise £250,000 to enable the Red Cross to reunite victims of the Civil War in Angola

102,537 bags raising over £1,000,000

TARGET	RESULT

2005 – The Treasure Trail Appeal
Enough old foreign coins and used mobile phones to pay for 5,000 extra calls to Childline

Enough funds raised to pay for an additional 151,000 calls

2006 – The Shoe Biz Appeal
500,000 pairs of shoes to help children orphaned by HIV and AIDS in Malawi

1,450,000 pairs of shoes including David Beckham's Real Madrid football boots! Helping 40,000 children

2007 – The Disc Drive Appeal
250,000 discs – CDs, DVDs and games consoles to fund 100,000 hours of support for young carers in the UK

502,000 discs providing funds for 1,000,000 hours of young carers' support

Christopher Trace, Valerie Singleton and John Noakes collecting paperback books for the 1966 Lifeboats Appeal

Acknowledgements

My grateful thanks to all the Blue Peter viewers who have contributed to this book and to Edward Barnes and Rosemary Gill without whose flair, enthusiasm and vision the "new" Blue Peter would never have set sail. Edward Barnes also created the Blue Peter Special Assignment series which added a valuable extra dimension to the programme.

Blue Peter would be nothing without its distinguished contributors especially Dorothy Smith, Margaret Parnell, Bob Broomfield, William Timyn, Percy Thrower, Derek Freeman and George Cansdale and the superb support of some memorable BBC bosses: Donald Baverstock, Alisdair Milne, Huw Wheldon, Ian Trethowan, Paul Fox, David Attenborough, Bill Cotton, Monica Sims and Michael Checkland. The contribution of the Presenters who created such a firm bond with the audience is inestimable.

I am indebted to Hazel Gill who transformed the Correspondence Unit, followed by Cilla Collar and Clemmie Chamberlain and my brilliant PAs: Angela Parish, Rosie Ferguson and Annie Dixon.

The film and studio directors all made a huge contribution: John Adcock, Alan Russell, Daniel Wolfe, Sarah Hellings, Renny Rye, David Brown, Rob Benfield, Tim Byford, David Langford, Michael Cook, Peter Brown and Alex Leger, as did editors Lewis Bronze, Oliver MacFarlane, Steve Hocking and Richard Marson.

I am grateful to Jack Lundie for his information about Blue Peter in the 21st Century and to Jacquie Kavanagh and her excellent team at the BBC Written Archives Centre.

This book would never have met its publishing deadline without Pat Spencer who not only deciphered my long hand but made invaluable comments. And without the support and encouragement of Emily, Rebecca, Vanessa and Aurea of Short Books, *Dear Blue Peter* would not have existed.